BRAIN ACADEMY
SUPERMATHS

Teacher's Book

Louise Moore and Pete Crawford

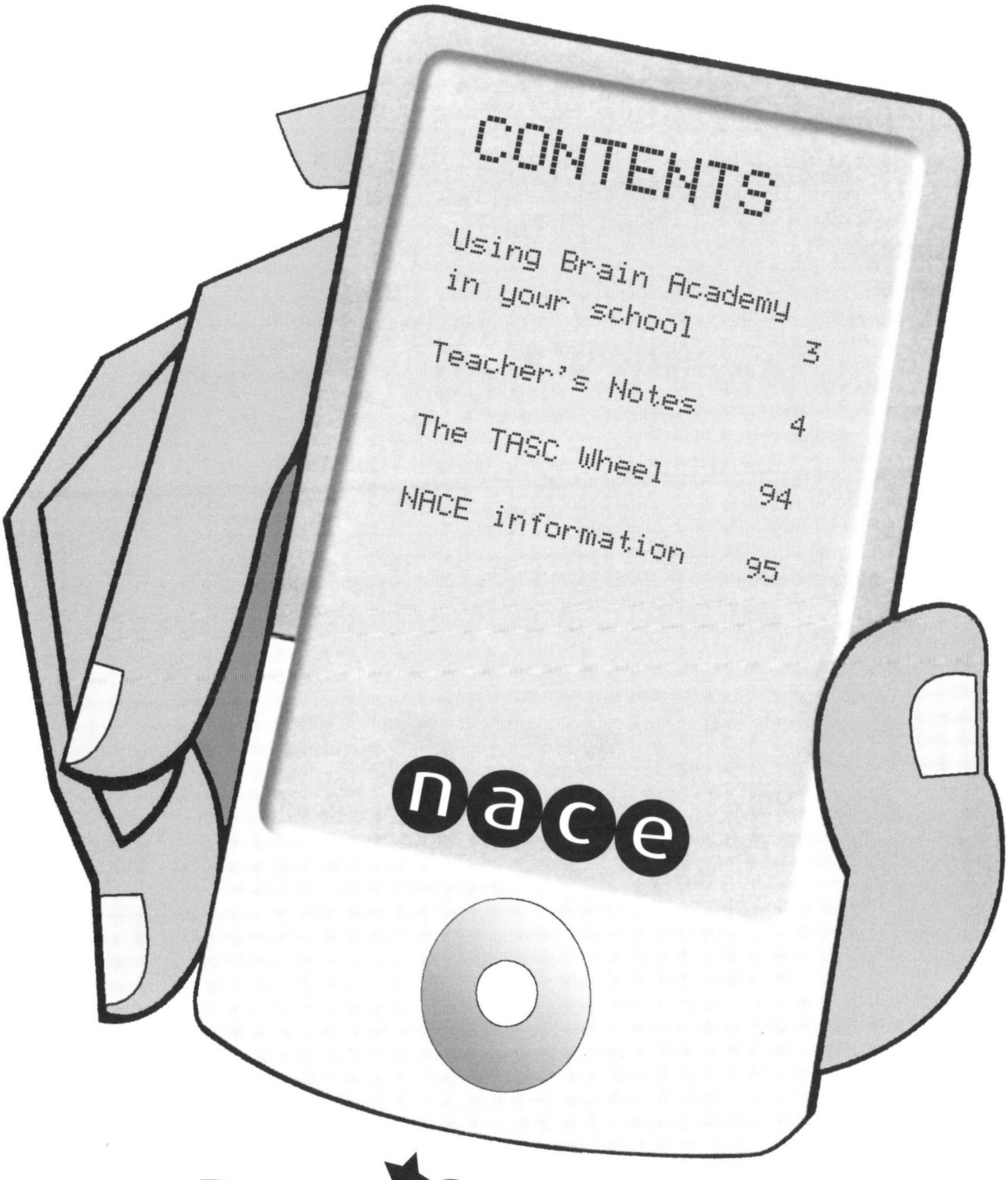

CONTENTS

Using Brain Academy in your school	3
Teacher's Notes	4
The TASC Wheel	94
NACE information	95

nace

RISING ★ STARS

Rising Stars are grateful to the following people for their support in developing this series: Sue Mordecai, Julie Fitzpatrick, Johanna Raffan, Belle Wallace and Clive Tunnicliffe.

NACE, PO Box 242, Arnolds Way, Oxford OX2 9FR
www.nace.co.uk

Rising Stars UK Ltd, 22 Grafton Street, London W1S 4EX
www.risingstars-uk.com

Every effort has been made to trace copyright holders and obtain their permission for the use of copyright materials. The authors and publisher will gladly receive information enabling them to rectify any error or omission in subsequent editions.

All facts are correct at time of going to press.

Published 2007
Text, design and layout © Rising Stars UK Ltd.

Editorial Consultant: Jean Carnall
Cover design: Burville-Riley
Design and layout: Pentacor**big**

All rights reserved. No part of this publication may be reproduced, stored in a retrieval system, or transmitted, in any form by any means, electronic, mechanical, photocopying, recording or otherwise, without the prior permission of Rising Stars.

British Library Cataloguing in Publication Data.
A CIP record for this book is available from the British Library.

ISBN: 978-1-84680-235-5

Printed by The Cromwell Press, Trowbridge, Wiltshire

USING BRAIN ACADEMY IN YOUR SCHOOL

Brain Academy Supermaths is a series of five books designed to provide a wealth of activities and investigations for your able, gifted and talented children. The activities are set in rich contexts that will enliven and enrich children's experience of maths.

A step-by-step approach to using Brain Academy Supermaths

1. Use the story and character conversation on the left hand page with your group or class. This helps introduce the topic in a fun and lively way.
2. Complete the Training Mission with your class or group. Using a whiteboard or flipchart will help here. This introduces the mathematical concepts to be covered in this mission.
3. Children can complete the Main Mission on their own, in pairs or groups, using the experience of the Training Mission.
4. Encourage children to use Huxley's Think Tank hints and the Mission Strategies to support independent learning.
5. Bring the group back together to share their experiences and results, and then set the Da Vinci Files as an investigation to be done either at home (if suitable) or work through the activity together.

Using the TASC Problem Solving Wheel

Thinking Actively in a Social Context: TASC is a well-researched universal thinking skills framework developed by Belle Wallace, President of NACE.

TASC empowers learners to:
- work independently yet within an inclusive school policy
- develop skills of research, investigation and problem-solving that can be used across the curriculum
- develop a positive sense of self as an active learner
- demonstrate their abilities using the full range of multiple intelligences
- develop skills of self-assessment.

TASC provides teachers with a framework for:
- lesson planning that systematically develops pupils' thinking
- effective planning for differentiation and extension
- a holistic approach to incorporating the multiple intelligences
- assessing the processes of pupils' learning.

To find out more about TASC, contact www.nace.co.uk.

Developing Brain Academy

If you are interested in developing Brain Academy by trialling, reviewing or writing more materials to cover other areas of the curriculum, please see our website www.risingstars-uk.com or email benbarton@risingstars-uk.com.

Mission File 1:1
Station spring clean

Primary Framework Strands
- Using and applying mathematics
- Handling data

Teaching Content
- Permutations
- Identifying patterns and relationships

Teacher's Notes

This is an excellent mission for developing systematic methods of working and recording work. It investigates permutations, so the order of the objects is significant (for example, red/blue is different to blue/red). You may wish to provide equipment so pupils can have practical experience of ordering and reordering objects.

The mission encourages pupils to realise that the number of permutations depends on the number of different objects.

TM

1 blue, red
red, blue (2 ways)

2 tea, coffee
coffee, tea (2 ways)

3 Buster Crimes, Inspector Pattern
Inspector Pattern, Buster Crimes (2 ways)

There are always 2 ways to order 2 items.

Pupils should devise sets that contain 2 different items and show 2 ways to order the items.

If the 2 items are the same there is only 1 way to order them.

Supermaths Book 1

MM

1 hammer, axe, saw   hammer, saw, axe
    axe, hammer, saw   axe, saw, hammer
    saw, hammer, axe   saw, axe, hammer
    (6 ways)

2 whistle, helmet, belt   whistle, belt, helmet
    helmet, whistle, belt   helmet, belt, whistle
    belt, whistle, helmet   belt, helmet, whistle
    (6 ways)

3 notebook, pen, telephone   notebook, telephone, pen
    pen, notebook, telephone   pen, telephone, notebook
    telephone, pen, notebook   telephone, notebook, pen
    (6 ways)

There are always 6 ways to order 3 items.

Pupils should devise sets that contain 3 different items and show 6 ways to order the items.

If 2 of the 3 are exactly the same, there are 3 orders (AAB, ABA, BAA).

If all 3 are exactly the same, there is only 1 order (AAA).

Da Vinci files

4 items the same gives 1 order.
AAAA

3 items the same and 1 different gives 4 orders.
AAAB   AABA   ABAA   BAAA
i.e. 1 x 4 = 4

2 items the same and 2 different gives 12 orders.
AABC   AACB   ABCA   ABAC   ACBA   ACAB
BAAC   BACA   BCAA   CBAA   CABA   CAAB
i.e. 1 x 4 x 3 = 12

4 different items gives 24 orders.
ABCD   ABDC   ACBD   ACDB   ADBC   ADCB   BACD   BADC   BCAD   BCDA   BDAC   BDCA
CABD   CADB   CBAD   CBDA   CDAB   CDBA   DABC   DACB   DBAC   DBCA   DCAB   DCBA
i.e. 1 x 4 x 3 x 2 = 24

Mission File 1:2

Dodgy dominoes

Primary Framework Strands
- Using and applying mathematics
- Knowing and using number facts
- Handling data

Teaching Content
- Addition and subtraction facts
- Identifying patterns and relationships

Teacher's Notes

This is a great mission for using number facts with which pupils are familiar. It includes visual reinforcement of the facts. Pupils have the opportunity to extend work on sequences by building a bank of results that can be analysed. The value of systematic and organised working can demonstrated with this mission. If you are short of sets of dominoes, it is possible to complete the mission with photocopies of sets.

Equipment: *sets of dominoes*

TM

1 Bazza cheats, Mrs Tiggles wins. The 6-6 domino has the greatest total (12), so Bazza could not have made a total of 14.

2 They all cheat! There are only 4 ways to make a total of 6 on the dominoes; 6-0, 5-1, 4-2, 3-3.

3 There are 6 ways to make a difference of 1 on the dominoes; 5-6, 4-5, 3-4, 2-3, 1-2, 0-1. Bazza wins and nobody cheats.

MM

1 Round one

Domino total	0	1	2	3	4	5	6
Ways to make the total	0-0	0-1	0-2 1-1	0-3 1-2	0-4 1-3 2-2	0-5 1-4 2-3	0-6 1-5 2-4 3-3
Number of ways	1	1	2	2	3	3	4

Domino total	7	8	9	10	11	12
Ways to make the total	1-6 2-5 3-4	2-6 3-5 4-4	3-6 4-5	4-6 5-5	5-6	6-6
Number of ways	3	3	2	2	1	1

2 Round two

Domino difference	0	1	2	3	4	5	6
Ways to make the difference	6-6 5-5 4-4 3-3 2-2 1-1 0-0	6-5 5-4 4-3 3-2 2-1 1-0	6-4 5-3 4-2 3-1 2-0	6-3 5-2 4-1 3-0	6-2 5-1 4-0	6-1 5-0	6-0
Number of ways	7	6	5	4	3	2	1

The number of ways keeps decreasing by 1.
The difference and the number of ways always total 7.

From each end of the set, the number of ways uses the pattern 1, 1, 2, 2, 3, 3 etc until it meets in the middle.

Supermaths Book 1

3 a) 1-spot

Domino difference	0	1
Ways to make the difference	1-1 0-0	0-1
Number of ways	2	1

The difference and the number of ways always total 2.

b) 2-spot

Domino difference	0	1	2
Ways to make the difference	2-2 1-1 0-0	2-1 0-1	2-0
Number of ways	3	2	1

The difference and the number of ways always total 3.

c) 3-spot

Domino difference	0	1	2	3
Ways to make the difference	3-3 2-2 1-1 0-0	3-2 2-1 0-1	3-1 2-0	3-0
Number of ways	4	3	2	1

The difference and the number of ways always total 4.

4-spot

Domino difference	0	1	2	3	4
Ways to make the difference	4-4 3-3 2-2 1-1 0-0	4-3 3-2 2-1 0-1	4-2 3-1 2-0	4-1 3-0	4-0
Number of ways	5	4	3	2	1

The difference and the number of ways always total 5.

5-spot

Domino difference	0	1	2	3	4	5
Ways to make the difference	5-5 4-4 3-3 2-2 1-1 0-0	5-4 4-3 3-2 2-1 0-1	5-3 4-2 3-1 2-0	5-2 4-1 3-0	5-1 4-0	5-0
Number of ways	6	5	4	3	2	1

The difference and the number of ways always total 6.

number of spots + 1 = difference + number of ways to make that difference

In a 9-spot set, the difference + number of ways would total 10. E.g. 7 dominoes in a 9-spot set have a difference of 3. (9-6, 8-5, 7-4, 6-3, 5-2, 4-1, 3-0)

Da Vinci files

1-spot

Domino total	0	1	2
Ways to make the total	0-0	0-1	1-1
Number of ways	1	1	1

2-spot

Domino total	0	1	2	3	4
Ways to make the total	0-0	0-1	0-2 1-1	1-2	2-2
Number of ways	1	1	2	1	1

3-spot

Domino total	0	1	2	3	4	5	6
Ways to make the total	0-0	0-1	0-2 1-1	0-3 1-2	1-3 2-2	2-3	3-3
Number of ways	1	1	2	2	2	1	1

4-spot

Domino total	0	1	2	3	4	5	6	7	8
Ways to make the total	0-0	0-1	0-2 1-1	0-3 1-2	0-4 1-3 2-2	1-4 2-3	2-4 3-3	3-4	4-4
Number of ways	1	1	2	2	3	2	2	1	1

5-spot

Domino total	0	1	2	3	4	5	6	7	8	9	10
Ways to make the total	0-0	0-1	0-2 1-1	0-3 1-2	0-4 1-3 2-2	0-5 1-4 2-3	1-5 2-4 3-3	2-5 3-4	3-5 4-4	4-5	5-5
Number of ways	1	1	2	2	3	3	3	2	2	1	1

From each end of the set, the number of ways uses the pattern 1, 1, 2, 2, 3, 3 etc until it meets in the middle.

10-spot dominoes give a range of totals from 0 to 20, so the number of ways will be 1, 1, 2, 2, 3, 3, 4, 4, 5, 5, 6, 5, 5, 4, 4, 3, 3, 2, 2, 1, 1.

Mission File 1:3
Amazing maps

Primary Framework Strands
- Using and applying mathematics
- Understanding shape

Teaching Content
- Position and direction

Teacher's Notes
This mission is an excellent opportunity to use and extend work on grids and directions.

Pupils will have to use compass directions to complete this mission.

Writing and sequencing directions are important elements of the set tasks.

TM

1 D1
2 A5
3 see completed grid
4 see completed grid
5 B2
6 C5
7 ball
8 sweet and/or bike
9 ball

	A	B	C	D	E
5	Bike		Sweet	Ball	
4			Sun		
3		Flag			
2		Face			
1				Pen	

A4 to pen, e.g. 3 East, 3 South or 2 South, 1 East, 1 South, 2 East

E1 to bike, e.g. 1 North, 2 West, 1 South, 2 West, 4 North or
2 North, 1 West, 2 South, 2 West, 3 North, 1 East, 1 North, 2 West

8 Supermaths Book 1

MM

1. a) E1 S2 W1 N1

   b) S2 (allow 1) E1 N1 E3 S2 W1 S1 W3 N1 E2 N1 E1

   c) N2 E3 S1 W2 S1 E2 (S1)

2. S2 (allow 1) E1 N1 E3 S2 W1 S1 W3 S2

3. S2 (allow 1) E1 N1 E3 S2 W1 S1 W3 N1 E2 N1 E1 (Dragon's Den)
   W1 S1 W2 S1 E3 N1 E1 N2 E1 S3 W1 (Enchanted Forest)

4. Allow any route that visits all the activity areas, e.g.
   S2 (allow 1) E1 N1 E4 S5 W1 N1 (Goblin's Garden)
   S1 E1 N2 W1 (Enchanted Forest)
   E1 N3 W1 S2 W1 S1 W3 N1 E2 N1 E1 (Dragon's Den)
   W1 S1 W2 S3 (Pixie Party)
   N2 E3 S1 W2 S1 E2 (S1)

Da Vinci files

Answers will vary for the children's own maze.

Mission File 1:4
Inspector Pattern's masterclass

Primary Framework Strands
- Using and applying mathematics
- Calculating

Teaching Content
- Addition and subtraction
- Identifying patterns and relationships

Teacher's Notes
The mission uses basic number bond knowledge to allow pupils to examine relationships between different sets in mathematics. Systematic working is encouraged and the analysis of results for patterns is central to this mission. There is something in this mission to challenge all pupils.

TM

1 3 + 5 = 8   5 + 3 = 8   8 − 3 = 5   8 − 5 = 3   (4 sums)

2 7 + 8 = 15   8 + 7 = 15   15 − 7 = 8   15 − 8 = 7   (4 sums)

3 Sets of cards where the total of 2 of the cards is the number on the third card, plus +, − and = cards

MM

1 0 + 3   1 + 2   2 + 1   3 + 0   (4 sums)

2 0 + 4   1 + 3   2 + 2   3 + 1   4 + 0   (5 sums)

3 0 + 5   1 + 4   2 + 3   3 + 2   4 + 1   5 + 0   (6 sums)

   0 + 6   1 + 5   2 + 4   3 + 3   4 + 2   5 + 1   6 + 0   (7 sums)

   0 + 7   1 + 6   2 + 5   3 + 4   4 + 3   5 + 2   6 + 1   7 + 0   (8 sums)

4

Answer	1	2	3	4	5	6	7	8
Number of sums you can make	2	3	4	5	6	7	8	9

The number of sums you can make is always 1 more than the answer to the sums.

The number of sums = answer + 1

12 sums for an answer of 11

Da Vinci files

Starting number	1	2	3	4	5	6	7	8
Number of sums you can make	2	3	4	5	6	7	8	9

The number of sums you can make is always 1 more than answer to the sums.

12 sums for starting number 11.

11 − 0 = 11   11 − 1 = 10   11 − 2 = 9   11 − 3 = 8   11 − 4 = 7   11 − 5 = 6
11 − 6 = 5   11 − 7 = 4   11 − 8 = 3   11 − 9 = 2   11 − 10 = 1 11 − 11 = 0

Mission File 1:5
Happy birthday, James!

Primary Framework Strands
- Using and applying mathematics
- Handling data

Teaching Content
- Combinations
- Identifying patterns and relationships

Teacher's Notes

This mission uses combinations of objects so the order doesn't matter (strawberry with chocolate is the same as chocolate with strawberry). By placing the tasks in fun contexts a careful investigation of all options is encouraged.

Results are collated to help pupils discover the rules involved.

TM

1 **a)** chocolate, chocolate   chocolate, mint   mint, mint   (3 choices)

   b) egg, egg   egg, jam   jam, jam   (3 choices)

   c) tuna, tuna   tuna, lamb   lamb, lamb   (3 choices)

   d) There are always 3 choices if you select 2 from 3 different options.

2 **a)** cherry, cherry   cherry, iced   cherry, currant
       iced, iced   iced, currant   currant, currant
       (6 choices)

   b) 2 balls   ball, string   ball, toy mouse
       2 strings   string, toy mouse   2 toy mice
       (6 choices)

MM

1 Picking 2 choices from 3 different options always gives 6 possible choices.
   There are 3 more choices (or twice as many) from 3 different options than from 2 different options.

2 hall, hall   hall, garden   hall, shed   hall, lounge   garden, garden
   garden, shed   garden, lounge   shed, shed   shed, lounge   lounge, lounge
   (10 choices)

3 There are always 10 possible choices when 2 things are picked from 4 different options.
   There are 4 more choices from 4 different options than from 3 different options.

Da Vinci files

Number of different colours	2	3	4	5	6
Number of ways to pick 2 bags	3	6	10	15	21
Difference to the pattern		+ 3	+ 4	+ 5	+ 6

The pattern keeps increasing the difference by 1, so 7 colours would have 21 + 7 = 28 choices.
The sequence 1, 3, 6, 10... is called the pattern of triangular numbers.

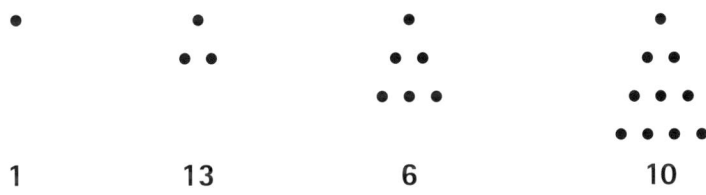

1   13   6   10

Mission File 1:6
Digital dilemma

Primary Framework Strands
- Using and applying mathematics
- Counting and understanding number

Teaching Content
- Place value

Teacher's Notes

This mission develops and consolidates understanding of place value. Pupils need a basic understanding of place value and knowledge of odd and even numbers to start this mission. They will be using this knowledge to develop investigative skills and working methods. The results generated are examined for patterns.

Equipment: *paper or card to make number cards*

TM

1 **a)** 86

   b) 35

   c) and **d)** 35, 36, 38, 53, 56, 58, 63, 65, 68, 83, 85, 86

2 **a)** 865

   b) 356

   c) and **d)**
   6 numbers from 356, 358, 365, 368, 385, 386, 536, 538, 563, 568, 583, 586, 635, 638, 653, 658, 683, 685, 835, 836, 853, 856, 863, 865

14   Supermaths Book 1

1 1, 15, 16, 156, 165, 5, 51, 56, 516, 561, 6, 61, 65, 615, 651

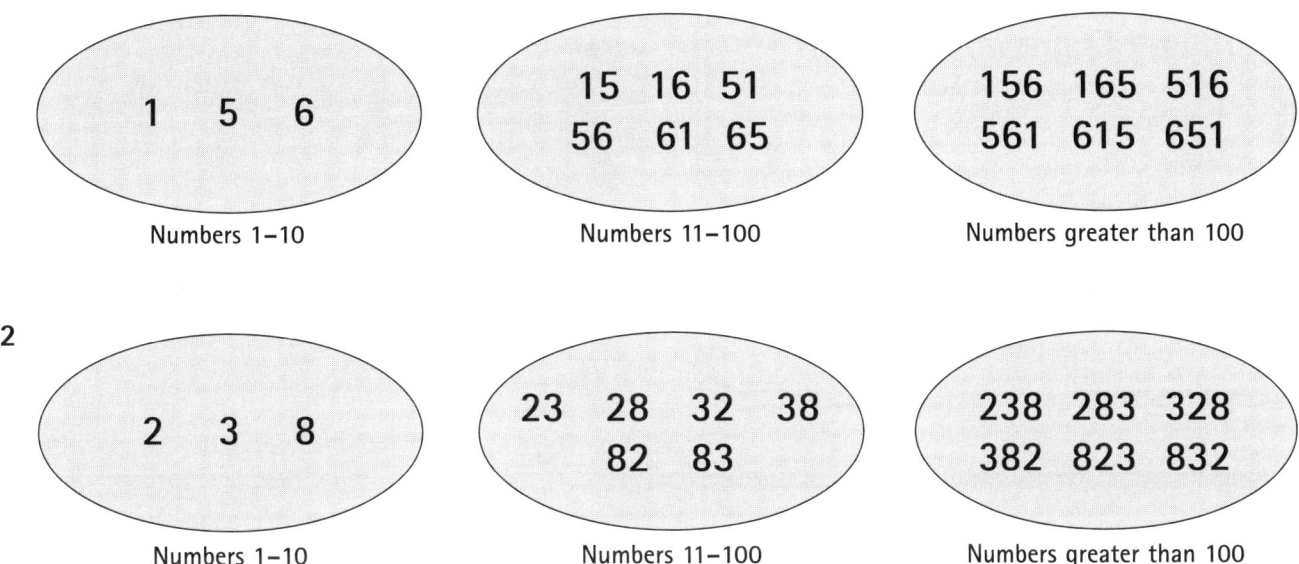

3 There are 3 numbers in the first group and 6 in the other two groups.

If 2 cards are the same, there are 2 numbers in the first group and 3 in the other two groups.

It doesn't matter which number is repeated.

If all 3 cards are the same, there is 1 number in each group.

4 a) 56, 66, 76

b) 55, 65, 75, 57, 67, 77

c) You made more odd numbers because there were 2 different odd numbers but only 1 even number.

Da Vinci files

You will need a selection of 3 digits that includes 2 or 3 different even numbers, all permutations correctly found.

A selection of 2 even and 2 odd digits will give the same amount of odd and even numbers. Either the 2 pairs must both be the same or they must both be different. If there are more odd digits than even, then more odd numbers can be made. If there are more even digits than odd, then more even numbers can be made.

Brain Academy Supermaths Teacher's Book   15

Mission File 1:7

Pie from the sky

Primary Framework Strands
- Using and applying mathematics
- Calculating
- Measuring

Teaching Content
- Telling the time (analogue and digital)

Teacher's Notes

As well as reinforcing analogue and digital times, this is a super mission for pupils to practise working out earlier and later times. The task extends into timetable work.

Pupils need to be able to recognise and add coins.

The mission allows pupils to develop both simple and complex patterns and codes, and use them in a fun context.

TM

1. **a)** 4 o' clock **b)** quarter past 5 **c)** quarter to 8 **d)** half past 10
   e) quarter to 10 **f)** 2 o' clock **g)** quarter to 3

2. **a)** 5 o' clock **b)** quarter past 6 **c)** quarter to 9 **d)** half past 11
   e) quarter to 11 **f)** 3 o' clock **g)** quarter to 4

3. **a)** half past 3 **b)** quarter to 5 **c)** quarter past 7 **d)** 10 o' clock
   e) quarter past 9 **f)** half past 1 **g)** quarter past 2

4. **a)** 4:00 **b)** 6:30 **c)** 8:45 **d)** 12:30
   e) 6:00 **f)** 7:45 **g)** 3:15

16   Supermaths Book 1

MM

1. For 5 minute intervals

1:45	2:35	3:25	4:15	5:05	5:50	6:40
7:30	8:20	9:10	10:45	11:35	12:25	

   (13 ways)

2. For 1 minute intervals

1:09	1:18	1:27	1:36	1:54	2:08	2:17	2:26	2:44	2:53	3:07
3:16	3:34	3:43	3:52	4:06	4:24	4:33	4:42	4:51	5:14	5:23
5:32	5:41	6:04	6:13	6:22	6:31	7:03	7:12	7:21	8:02	8:11
9:01	10:09	10:18	10:27	10:36	10:54	2:08	11:17	11:26	11:44	11:53
12:07	12:16	12:34	12:43	12:52						

   (49 more ways, giving a total of 62 altogether)

3. For example:

   Clock 1 says 1:10 = 1 + 1 + 0 = 2 hours
   Clock 2 says 8:25 = 8 + 2 + 5 = 15 minutes
   That gives 2:15.

   Any examples that fit this model are correct.

   The largest number you can make is for 9:59 = 9 + 5 + 9 = 23, so you can't have more than 23 minutes past the hour.

4. You should be able to construct any time with this method.

Da Vinci files

Answers will vary. Pupils should produce a timetable using the code in Q4 from the MM.

Mission File 1:8

Happy birthday, Mr President!

Primary Framework Strands
- Using and applying mathematics
- Handling data

Teaching Content
- Tallies
- Venn diagrams

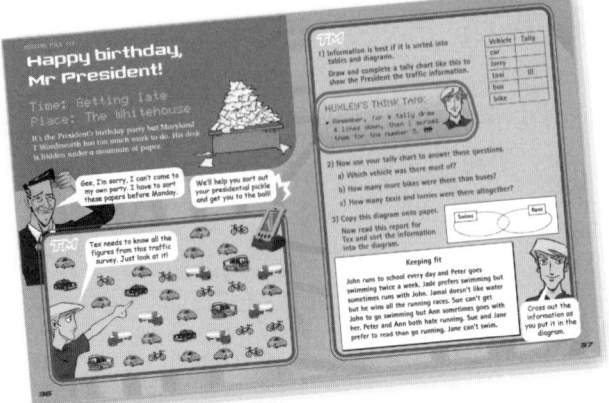

Teacher's Notes

Venn diagrams are great vehicles for logic problems and there are some tricky number problems in this mission that will delight bright pupils. The logic problems can be extremely satisfying to solve.

Pupils will need to use information about friends for the Da Vinci files. If this is a problem, give pupils a bank of information – perhaps pages from a catalogue or some photos – and let them use those to gather the required information.

TM

1

Vehicle	Tally
Car	╫╫ ╫╫ ‖‖‖ (14)
Lorry	╫╫ (5)
Taxi	‖‖ (3)
Bus	‖ (1)
Bike	╫╫ ‖‖‖ (9)

2 **a)** car   **b)** 8   **c)** 8

3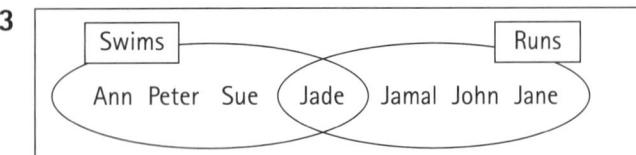

MM

1 Buster Crimes ╫╫ ‖‖ (8)   Sandy Bucket ‖ (1)   Inspector Pattern ‖ (1)
   Buster Crimes ╫╫ ‖ (6)   Sandy Bucket ‖‖ (2)   Inspector Pattern ‖‖ (2)
   Buster Crimes ‖‖‖ (4)   Sandy Bucket ‖‖‖ (3)   Inspector Pattern ‖‖‖ (3)

18 Supermaths Book 1

2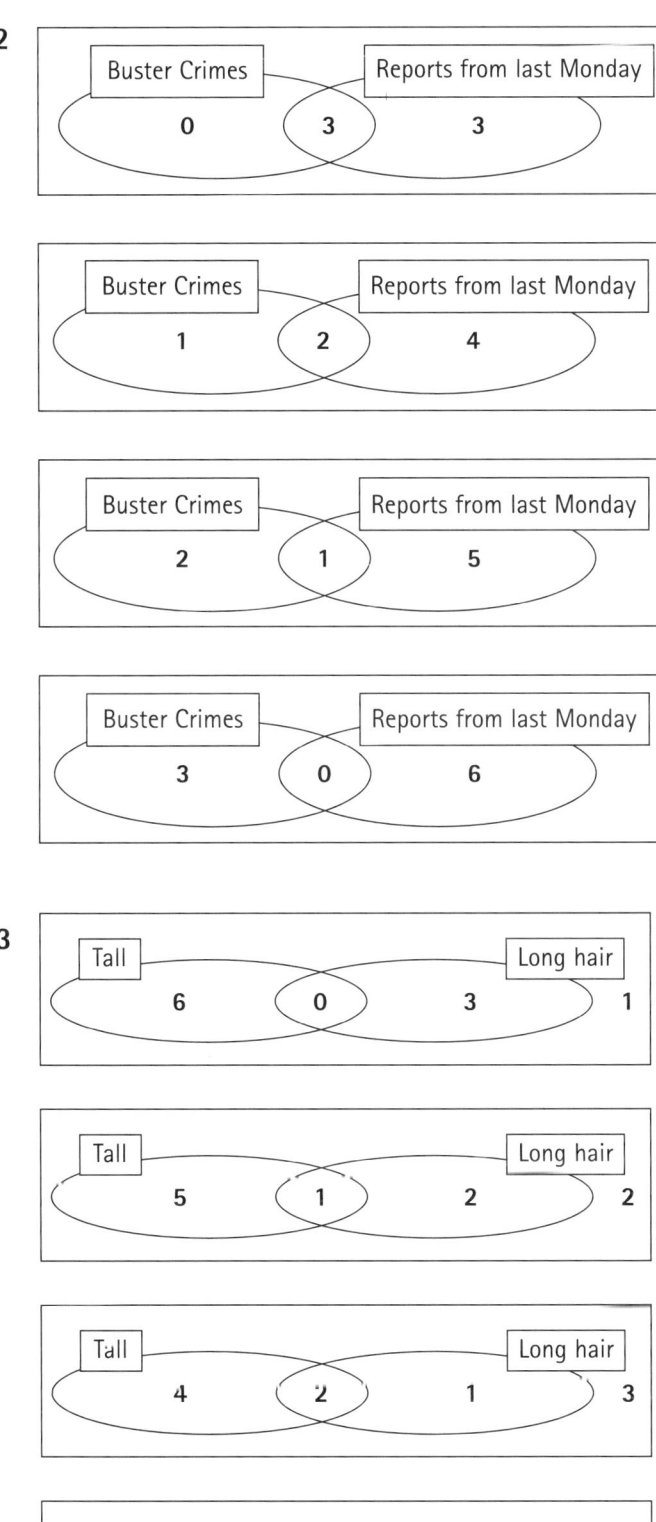

3

Tall		Long hair	
6	0	3	1

Tall		Long hair	
5	1	2	2

Tall		Long hair	
4	2	1	3

Tall		Long hair	
3	3	0	4

Da Vinci files

Answers will vary. Pupils should show their own diagram(s) with information about friends, e.g. foods, pets, physical characteristics, hobbies.

Mission File 1:9

Nobbled by the Nibblers!

Primary Framework Strands
- Using and applying mathematics
- Calculating
- Measuring

Teaching Content
- Number patterns and relationships

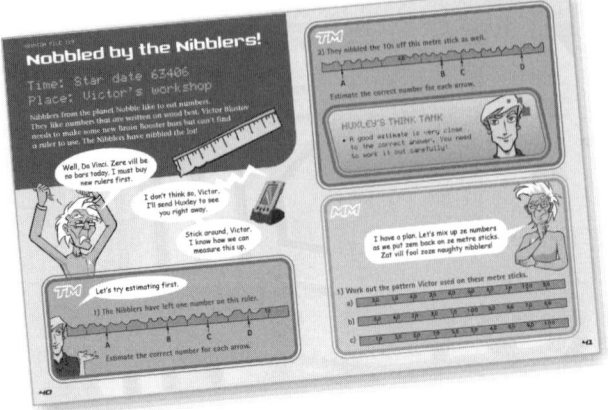

Teacher's Notes

Place value, number lines and sequences are all incorporated into this interesting mission. There is plenty of scope for practical work as well as recording. If number rods are available, some pupils might benefit from this additional equipment (though the mission can be successfully completed without such equipment).

Extension using different length rods and different target numbers is possible – pupils could even devise additional challenges themselves.

TM

1) A = 2, B = 5, C = 7, D = 9

2) A = 10, B = 60, C = 70, D = 100

MM

1. **a)** Each pair of numbers has been swapped round, so 10 swapped with 20, 30 swapped with 40 and so on.

   b) The first 5 numbers have been written in reverse order and the last 5 numbers have been written in reverse order.

   c) The numbers with an odd tens digit have been written in ascending order, followed by the numbers with even tens digits written in ascending order.

2. **a)** Add 5   **b)** Add 20   **c)** Take away 4   **d)** Add 12

3. **a)** Add 1, add 3   **b)** Take away 2, add 2

4. Answers will vary. Check the sequences against the rule chosen.

Supermaths Book 1

Da Vinci files

1 = 5 + 5 + 5 − 7 − 7
2 = 7 − 5
3 = 5 + 5 − 7
4 = 7 + 7 − 5 − 5
5 = 5
6 = 7 + 7 + 7 − 5 − 5 − 5
7 = 7
8 = 5 + 5 + 5 − 7
9 = 7 + 7 − 5
10 = 5 + 5

1 = 9 − 3 − 5	11 = 5 + 3 + 3
2 = 5 − 3	12 = 9 + 3
3 = 3	13 = 5 + 5 + 3
4 = 9 − 5	14 = 9 + 5
5 = 5	15 = 5 + 5 + 5
6 = 3 + 3	16 = 5 + 5 + 3 + 3
7 = 9 − 5 + 3	17 = 9 + 3 + 5
8 = 5 + 3	18 = 9 + 9
9 = 9	19 = 5 + 5 + 9
10 = 5 + 5	20 = 5 + 5 + 5 + 5

Note that there are alternative answers for many of these. Finding them could be an extra challenge.

Mission File 2:1

Piping problem for Sandy

Primary Framework Strands
- Using and applying mathematics
- Knowing and using number facts
- Calculating

Teaching Content
- Combinations
- Number bonds
- Addition

Teacher's Notes

Encourage children to take a systematic approach when tackling questions that ask them to find all the ways of making different lengths. So maybe start with 1 length and add all the other lengths one at a time in turn. Then, start with 2 lengths and add all the other lengths 1 at a time in turn, and so on, looking out for repeats.

When making their own sets of pipes, the ones that give the greatest lengths whilst still managing all lengths are the lengths that are the base 2 column headings – 1, 2, 4, 8 and so on.

Equipment: *cubes*

TM

1 a) 1 + 5 or 2 + 4

b) 7 + 5 or 7 + 4 + 1 or 9 + 2 + 1 or 5 + 4 + 2 + 1

2 shortest = 1, longest = 28

3

Length 1	1
Length 2	2
Length 3	3, 1 + 2
Length 4	4, 3 + 1
Length 5	2 + 3, 1 + 4
Length 6	1 + 2 + 3, 2 + 4
Length 7	4 + 3, 4 + 2 + 1
Length 8	4 + 3 + 1
Length 9	4 + 3 + 2
Length 10	1 + 2 + 3 + 4

MM

1 a) shortest = 1   **b)** longest = 17

c)

Length 1	1
Length 2	2
Length 3	1 + 2
Length 4	
Length 5	5
Length 6	5 + 1
Length 7	5 + 2
Length 8	5 + 2 + 1
Length 9	9
Length 10	9 + 1
Length 11	9 + 2
Length 12	9 + 2 + 1
Length 13	
Length 14	9 + 5
Length 15	9 + 5 + 1
Length 16	9 + 5 + 2
Length 17	9 + 5 + 2 + 1

2 The following sets will all give all values between 1 and the longest and make more pipes than Sandy's:

1, 2, 3, 5   1, 2, 3, 6   1, 2, 3 7   1, 2, 4, 5
1, 2, 4, 6   1, 2, 4, 7   1, 2, 4, 8

3 1, 2, 4, 8 is the set that gives the longest possible pipe and still makes all the lengths.

Da Vinci files

The shortest length is 1, the longest is 25.
Not all lengths are possible.

Length	
1	1
2	
3	3
4	3 + 1
5	5
6	6, 5 + 1
7	6 + 1
8	5 + 3
9	6 + 3, 5 + 3 + 1, 10 + 5 + 1
10	6 + 3 + 1
11	10 + 1, 6 +5
12	6 + 5 + 1
13	10 + 3
14	10 + 3 + 1, 6 + 5 + 3
15	10 + 5, 6 + 5 + 3 + 1
16	10 + 6
17	10 + 6 + 1
18	10 + 5 + 3
19	10 + 5 + 3 + 1
20	10 + 6 + 3 + 1
21	10 + 6 + 5
22	10 + 6 + 5 + 1
23	
24	10 + 6 + 5 + 3
25	10 + 6 + 5 + 3 + 1

1, 2, 4, 8, 16 is the set that gives the longest possible pipe (31) and still makes all the lengths.

Brain Academy Supermaths Teacher's Book

Mission File 2:2

Tessa, late? No, she made it just in time!

Primary Framework Strands
- Using and applying mathematics
- Understanding shape

Teaching Content
- Tessellation
- Properties of 2D shapes

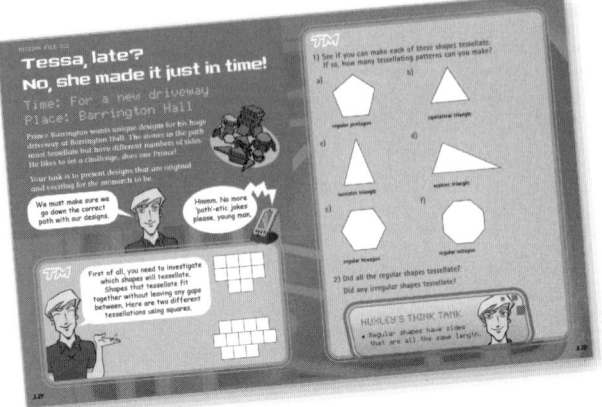

Teacher's Notes

This mission is great as a tool for encouraging accurate and careful drawing of shapes. Through an investigation of creating tessellating shapes, children consolidate other shape knowledge.

Pupils will need lots of large (probably about A3) sheets of paper for testing different shapes.

To complete the Da Vinci files, children will need to find a way to create shapes that tessellate and have an odd number of sides. They can do this by using an equilateral triangle as the base shape (see answers for further instructions).

It is possible to extend this investigation by examining angle sums around each point in tessellating shapes.

Equipment: *plastic 2D shapes, card, scissors, sticky tape, large sheets of paper*

TM

1 a) will not tessellate

b) tessellates; multiple offset patterns possible

c) tessellates; number of patterns depends on the sizes of the angles used

d) tessellates; number of patterns depends on the sizes of the angles used

e) tessellates; one way

f) will not tessellate

2 Not all regular shapes tessellate. Some irregular shapes tessellate.

MM

1 Tessellation, using octagons

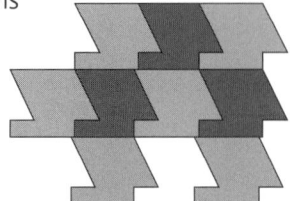

24   Supermaths Book 2

2 Any triangle cut from 1 corner to an adjacent corner will work. For example:

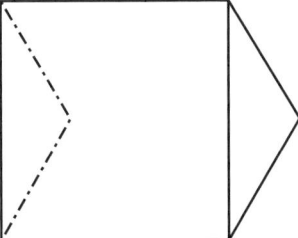

3 For example:

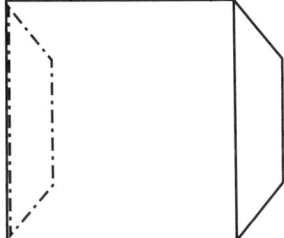

4 Can be done with a 3, 4, or 5-sided shape cut from one side.

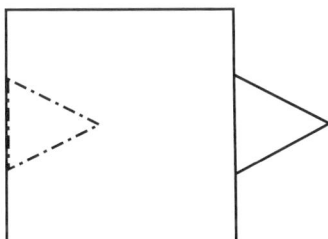 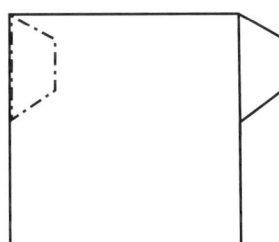 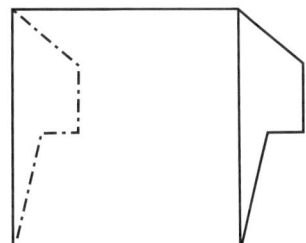

Da Vinci files

Cutting different shapes from the sides will give a wide variety of new shapes. For example, cutting a 6-sided shape from 1 side and sticking it to the other could give a shape with 12, 14 or 16 sides, and the shape will tessellate.

All shapes have an even number of sides. You can't use this method to make a tessellating shape with an odd number of sides. By sticking on the shape you cut off, you are doubling the number of extra sides you make, and doubled numbers are always even.

Using an equilateral triangle as the base shape will allow you to make tessellating shapes with an odd number of sides.

 For example, this gives a 5-sided tessellating shape.

Children may design paths with a row of 3-sided tessellating shapes, then 4-sided, then 5-sided, 6-sided and so on.

Mission File 2:3
Digital watch

Primary Framework Strands
- Using and applying mathematics
- Counting and understanding number
- Calculating

Teaching Content
- Place value
- Addition, subtraction, multiplication

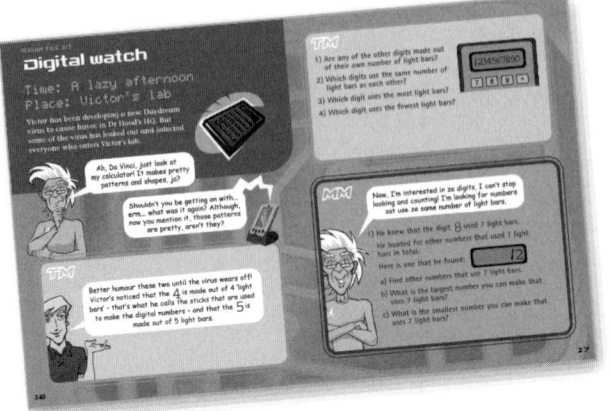

Teacher's Notes

It is helpful to look at the way digital numbers are formed before starting this, agreeing on the way that 7 and 9 are made as these numbers can be made differently on different displays.

When looking for the highest number with a given number of light bars, see if the children recognise that sometimes a small digit in a higher column is more useful than a large digit in a lower column.

The multiplication in question 3) c) might give rise to fractions or decimals (e.g. $9\frac{1}{2} \times 4 = 38$). Such thinking should be encouraged!

Equipment: *lolly sticks or matchsticks*

TM

Number	1	2	3	4	5	6	7	8	9	0
Number of light bars	2	5	5	4	5	6	3	7	6	6

1 6 uses six light bars

2 2, 3 and 5 all use 5 light bars
   6, 9 and 0 all use 6 light bars

3 8 uses 7 light bars

4 1 uses 2 light bars

MM

1 a) Possible numbers are: 8, 12, 13, 15, 21, 31, 47, 51, 74, 117, 171, 711

   b) 711

   c) 8

26   Supermaths Book 2

2 a) Possible numbers are: 10, 16, 19, 27, 37, 44, 57, 61, 72, 73, 75, 91, 114, 141, 411, 177, 717, 771, 1111

   b) 1111

   c) 10 (unless children argue for 01, as used in dates etc.)

3 a) There are many possible additions where the answer is 38, e.g. 18 + 15 + 5

   b) There are many possible subtractions where the answer is 38, e.g. 62 − 24

   c) There are the 2 whole number multiplications that give the answer 38:
   1 × 38 and 2 × 19
   Some children may give others such as $\frac{1}{2}$ × 76

4 There are many possible answers to this. Check for a correct calculation that gives an answer that uses 12 light bars, e.g. 9 × 10 = 90

5 Check that the children's answers each use 10 light bars and then check for correct calculations that give their numbers.

Da Vinci files

There are many possible times that use 14 light bars, e.g. 4:25 p.m.

Mission File 2:4

Round and round and round...

Primary Framework Strands
- Using and applying mathematics
- Knowing and using number facts

Teaching Content
- Factors
- Square numbers
- Number pattern
- Reasoning

Teacher's Notes

The TM could be developed to look at factors of other numbers and include prime numbers should you wish. Questions could include: What arrangements could Inspector Pattern make with 24 buttons? What about 36 or 17 buttons? Of these, 17 will only allow a single row, which Inspector Pattern does not want. What other numbers will cause her the same problem?

For the MM, suggest that the children make and list the first few square numbers in order. They could use counters to represent the buttons. They should then be able to use their list to find suitable combinations of square numbers.

The Da Vinci files give room for more reasoning and proof. See the answers for more detail.

TM

1 6

2 2 rows of 9, 3 rows of 6, 9 rows of 2, 6 rows of 3

3 2 rows of 10, 4 rows of 5, 5 rows of 4, 10 rows of 2

MM

1 9

2 5

3 2 × 2, 3 × 3, 4 × 4, 5 × 5, 6 × 6, 7 × 7, 8 × 8, 9 × 9

4 There are several ways of achieving this including:

10 squares of 9 buttons

1 square of 9 and 1 square of 81

1 square of 4, 1 square of 16 and 2 squares of 25

2 squares of 9 and 2 squares of 36

6 squares of 9 and 1 square of 36

1 square of each of 49, 25 and 16

Others may be possible.

If children have included 1 as a square, then other ways are definitely possible.

5 see above

Da Vinci Files

3

5

7

9

The number Inspector Pattern adds keeps increasing by 2 and is always odd.

She is right. The difference between consecutive square numbers is always an odd number. If children say that it always happens simply because it has happened with the examples they have tried, push them to give a reason why it will always happen, however many examples they try. One way of showing this is as follows:

Look at the buttons that are being added each time. Each time you add buttons, you place the same number along the top edge and the right-hand side of the previous square (the black buttons below), and then 1 more in the top right corner:

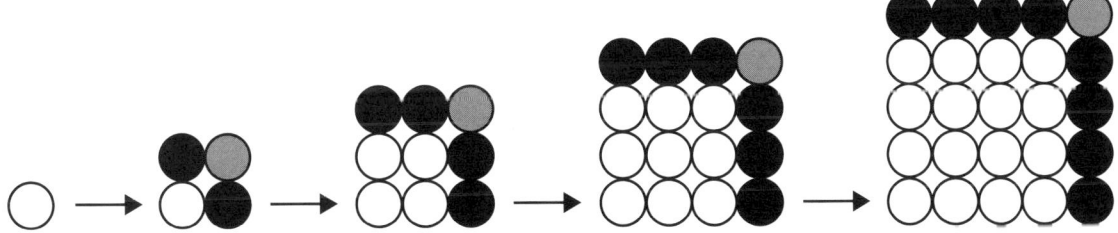

The black buttons must always be an even number, as they are 2 lots of the same number. Then the grey button is added, so the total number added must be 1 more than an even number, which must be odd.

Brain Academy Supermaths Teacher's Book

Mission File 2:5

Square-count cat?

Primary Framework Strands
- Using and applying mathematics

Teaching Content
- Number patterns
- Prediction

Teacher's Notes

Encourage children to work systematically, maybe by finding all the small squares first, then all of the next-sized squares and so on up to the largest square.

Talk about the patterns in the numbers. Encourage children to use these patterns to predict the next results before drawing them.

Children should use pattern in a similar way to solve the Da Vinci files. If they make a table for the patchworks that are shown, they should be able to extend it without drawing any (or at least many) more patchworks.

Equipment: *squared paper*

TM

1 a) 6   b) 2   c) 8

2 a) 8   b) 3   c) 11

3 14

MM

1 a) The number of small squares increases by 2 each time.

   The number of big squares increases by 1 each time.

   The total number of squares increases by 3 each time.

   b) 12   c) 5   d) 17   e) Children check by drawing and counting.

2 14 (9 small, 4 medium, 1 big)

3

Length of patchwork	3	4	5
Number of small squares	9	12	15
Number of medium squares	4	6	8
Number of big squares	1	2	3
Total number of squares	14	20	26

Supermaths Book 2

4   32 (18 small, 10 medium, 4 big)

5   38 (21 small, 12 medium, 5 big)

6   Children check by drawing and counting.

7   56 (30 small, 18 medium, 8 big)

Da Vinci Files

Jemima's patchwork has a length of 11.

Some children might answer 25 as 25 × 4 = 100, but that would only count the small squares. Jemima's patchworks contain four different sizes of square:

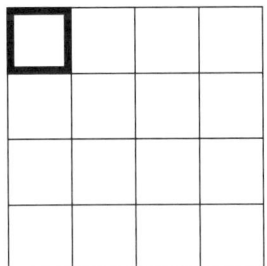 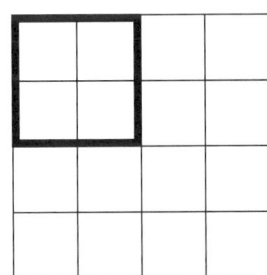 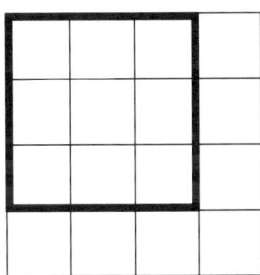 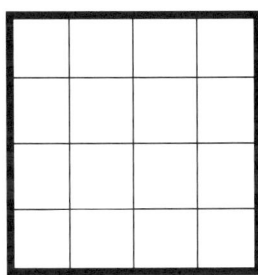

Brain Academy Supermaths Teacher's Book

Mission File 2:6

Time flies (if you throw your watch out of the window!)

Primary Framework Strands
- Using and applying mathematics
- Calculating
- Measuring

Teaching Content
- Time
- Addition

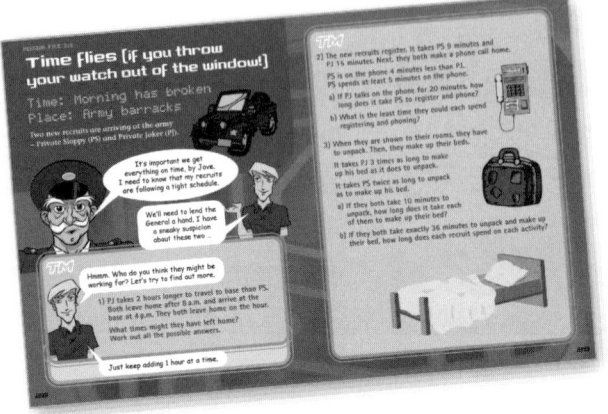

Teacher's Notes

In a fun context, children have to manipulate lengths of time and combine timetables for 2 people to fulfil given criteria.

Encourage the children to consider all the possible solutions by starting with the shortest (or longest) possible time and working up (or down).

When making up their own problems, emphasise that children need to keep checking that they give enough information (or solutions will be impossible to find), and that they don't give too much information (or the solutions will be incredibly easy to find).

1

| PS | 11 a.m. | noon | 1 p.m. | 2 p.m. | 3 p.m. |
| PJ | 9 a.m. | 10 a.m. | 11 a.m. | noon | 1 p.m. |

2 a) 25 minutes

   b) PS: 14 minutes, PJ: 24 minutes

3 a) PJ: 30 minutes, PS: 5 minutes

   b) PJ: bed 27 minutes, unpack 9 minutes
      PS: bed 12 minutes, unpack 24 minutes

32   Supermaths Book 2

MM

a) PJ: 6:28, PS: 6:25

b) 5 minutes

c)

PJ	6:28	6:30	6:32	6:34	6:36	6:38	6:40	6:42	6:44	6:46	6:48	6:50
PS	6:25	6:28	6:31	6:34	6:37	6:40	6:43	6:46	6:49	6:52	6:55	6:58

d) PJ: 4:38 a.m.
PS: 4:42 a.m. (plus 30 seconds)

Da Vinci files

Answers will vary. Check the problems and solutions.

Mission File 2:7

Button holes for Victor

Primary Framework Strands
- Using and applying mathematics
- Calculating

Teaching Content
- Addition, subtraction
- Mental strategies

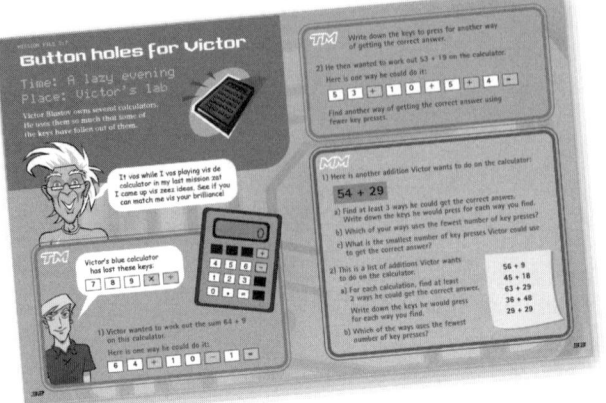

Teacher's Notes

Many of the questions allow discussion of adjusted calculations that can be useful mental strategies. For example, the questions that add 9, 19, 29 and so on lend themselves to the add 10 and take away 1 approach. This can be developed for adding 8, 18, 28 etc.

When the children adapt the approach for subtraction, do they realise that they need to add the adjustment? E.g. 43 − 29 = 43 − 30 + 1

With questions such as 4) b), the equal addition approach can be discussed, where the same number is added to both parts of the subtraction to keep the difference the same, e.g. 75 − 42 becomes 77 − 44. Discuss uses of this. For example, when subtracting 38 from 56, which do the children find easier to work out mentally, 56 − 38 or 58 − 40? Why do they both have the same answer?

TM

1 There are many possible ways e.g. 64 + 5 + 4 =

2 One way using fewer key presses is: 53 + 20 − 1 =
There may be other ways.

MM

1 a) Children will have different ways. The following show 3 possibilities:

54 + 30 − 1 =   54 + 20 + 6 + 3 =   53 + 30 =

b) Depends on answers to **a)**.

c) 54 + 30 − 1 = uses 8 presses. Some children might have adjusted the question and used 53 + 30 = which takes 7 presses.

34   Supermaths Book 2

2 a) and **b)**

Children may have different ways of answering these. Here are some possibilities:

56 + 10 − 1 = is an efficient mental method. However 56 + 6 + 3 = uses 1 fewer key presses.

45 + 10 + 6 + 2 =   45 + 20 − 2 =   use fewer key presses.

63 + 30 − 1 = is 1 way. Another is to take 1 from the 63 and give it to the 29 to do 62 + 30 =

36 + 50 − 2 =   36 + 40 + 4 + 4 =   34 + 50 =   use fewer key presses.

30 − 1 + 30 + 1 =   30 + 30 − 2 =   use fewer key presses.

3 a) and **b)**

Again, many answers are possible, some more efficient than others.

43 − 10 + 1 = is an efficient mental method. However 43 − 5 − 4 = uses 1 fewer key presses.

61 − 10 − 5 − 4 =   61 − 20 + 1 =   use fewer key presses.

Some children may be tempted to try 60 − 20 by using the 1 from the 61 with the 19. If they do, then discuss why this might work with addition but not with subtraction.

55 − 10 − 6 − 2 =   55 − 20 + 2 =   use fewer key presses.

60 − 30 + 3 =   60 − 20 − 4 − 3 =   63 − 30 =   use fewer key presses.

4 Many answers are possible, some more efficient than others.

54 + 50 − 9 = is a variation of the mental strategy for adding 9, 19, 29 and so on. However, adjusting the sum to 55 + 40 = requires fewer key presses.

75 − 50 + 8 =   77 − 44 =
would have the same difference as both numbers are 2 more than the originals.

87 + 40 − 7 = is 1 way. Some children might want to turn it into 90 + 30 and then find that 30 is not directly possible. However, 80 + 40 = can be done and is an efficient adjustment in this case.

Da Vinci files

Many answers are possible, some more efficient than others. Check individual methods.

Mission File 2:8
Giggles at bedtime

Primary Framework Strands
- Using and applying mathematics
- Counting and understanding number
- Calculating

Teaching Content
- Addition, subtraction
- Patterns and rules

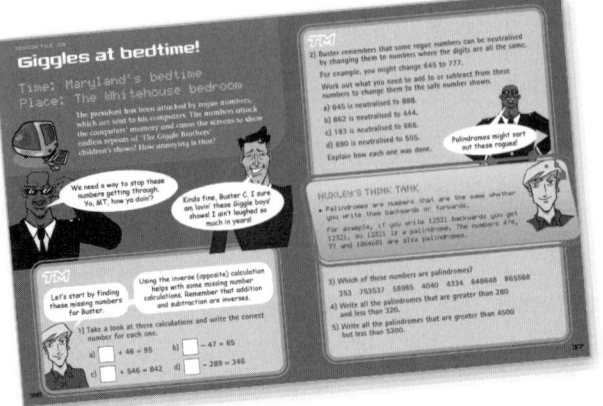

Teacher's Notes

Palindromes are the focus of this mission, so it essential that children have a clear understanding of palindromes at the end of the training mission.

Using conditions and limitations, children have to find palindromes to solve problems. Encourage (but try not to direct) a systematic approach to each problem, as children need to find all the solutions if they are to establish any patterns and rules at the end of the mission.

TM

1 a) 49   b) 112   c) 296   d) 635

2 a) add 243   b) subtract 418 c) add 473   d) subtract 135

3 353   58985   4334   865568

4 282   292   303   313

5 4554   4664   4774   4884   4994   5005   5115   5225

MM

1 a) 68 + 9 = 77   68 + 20 = 88   68 + 31 = 99

   b) 68 − 2 = 66   68 − 13 = 55   68 − 24 = 44
      68 − 35 = 33   68 − 46 = 22   68 − 57 = 11

   c) 9 ways

2 45 + 10 = 55   45 + 21 = 66   45 + 32 = 77   45 + 43 = 88   45 + 54 = 99
   45 + 1 = 44   45 − 12 = 33   45 − 23 = 22   45 − 34 = 11
   (9 ways)

3 59 + 7 = 66   59 + 18 = 77   59 + 29 = 88   59 + 40 = 99   59 − 4 = 55
   59 − 15 = 44   59 − 26 = 33   59 − 37 = 22   59 − 48 = 11
   (9 ways)

Supermaths Book 1

4 There are always 9 solutions to this problem as there are 9 2-digit palindromes.

5 No. Changing 2 digits to 3 means using a multiple of 10 not 100. Also there are 10 palindromes between 100 and 200, so there will be 10 for each 100 from 100 up to 900, which gives 90 palindromes.

Da Vinci files

Digit sum of 674 is 17. Odd palindromes with a digit sum of 17 are 737 and 575. (2 ways)

Digit sum of 325 is 10. Even palindromes with a digit sum of 10 are 262 and 424. (2 ways)

Mission File 2:9

Breaking news... world's chocolate reserves melting fast!

Primary Framework Strands
- Using and applying mathematics
- Counting and understanding number
- Knowing and using number facts
- Calculating

Teaching Content
- Fractions

Teacher's Notes

Fractions are presented visually in this mission. When talking with the children, emphasise that each type of fraction (e.g. all the thirds) need to have the same area, and that they are easier to identify if they are the same shape as well.

Accurate cutting is required and children should be encouraged to check rigorously (so extra paper is quite likely to be needed)!

When looking for rules and patterns, children need to consider relationships that involve multiplication and division.

Equipment: *about eight 6 x 6 pieces of squared paper for each group or child*

TM

Check the fractional pieces are made correctly.

MM

1 a) 3   b) 4   c) $\frac{2}{2}$ $\frac{3}{3}$ $\frac{4}{4}$ $\frac{6}{6}$ $\frac{8}{8}$ $\frac{12}{12}$

   d) The top and bottom numbers (numerator and denominator) are the same when a fraction is equal to 1.

2

Fractions that are the same as $\frac{1}{2}$	Fractions that don't match $\frac{1}{2}$
$\frac{2}{4}, \frac{3}{6}, \frac{4}{8}, \frac{6}{12}$	$\frac{1}{3}$

The bottom number (denominator) must be double the top number (numerator).

denominator ÷ numerator = 2

3

Fractions that are the same as $\frac{1}{3}$	Fractions that don't match $\frac{1}{3}$
$\frac{2}{6}$ $\frac{4}{12}$	$\frac{1}{2}$ $\frac{1}{4}$ $\frac{1}{8}$

The bottom number (denominator) must be triple the top number (numerator).

Denominator ÷ numerator = 3

4

Fractions that are the same as $\frac{1}{4}$	Fractions that don't match $\frac{1}{4}$
$\frac{2}{8}$ $\frac{3}{12}$	$\frac{1}{2}$ $\frac{1}{3}$ $\frac{1}{6}$

The bottom number (denominator) must be quadruple the top number (numerator).

denominator ÷ numerator = 4

Supermaths Book 1

5 In equivalent fractions, the ratio between the top and bottom numbers is the same/the top and bottom numbers have been multiplied by the same number/dividing the denominator by the numerator in 1 fraction gives the same answer as dividing the denominator by the numerator in the other fraction.

Da Vinci files

Equivalent fractions are listed systematically here for reference, although children are unlikely to do it like this. They may instead start separate chains, e.g. for $\frac{1}{6}, \frac{2}{6}, \frac{3}{6}, \frac{4}{6}, \frac{5}{6}$ and not realise that $\frac{2}{6}, \frac{3}{6}$ and $\frac{4}{6}$ will have already been included in the chains for $\frac{1}{3}, \frac{2}{3}$ and $\frac{1}{2}$ respectively.

$\frac{1}{2} = \frac{2}{4} = \frac{3}{6} = \frac{4}{8} = \frac{5}{10} = \frac{6}{12} = \frac{7}{14} = \frac{8}{16} = \frac{9}{18} = \frac{10}{20} = \frac{11}{22} = \frac{12}{24} = \frac{13}{26} = \frac{14}{28} = \frac{15}{30}$

$\frac{1}{3} = \frac{2}{6} = \frac{3}{9} = \frac{4}{12} = \frac{5}{15} = \frac{6}{18} = \frac{7}{21} = \frac{8}{24} = \frac{9}{27} = \frac{10}{30}$

$\frac{2}{3} = \frac{4}{6} = \frac{6}{9} = \frac{8}{12} = \frac{10}{15} = \frac{12}{18} = \frac{14}{21} = \frac{16}{24} = \frac{18}{27} = \frac{20}{30}$

$\frac{1}{4} = \frac{2}{8} = \frac{3}{12} = \frac{4}{16} = \frac{5}{20} = \frac{6}{24} = \frac{7}{28}$

$\frac{3}{4} = \frac{6}{8} = \frac{9}{12} = \frac{12}{16} = \frac{15}{20} = \frac{18}{24} = \frac{21}{28}$

$\frac{1}{5} = \frac{2}{10} = \frac{3}{15} = \frac{4}{20} = \frac{5}{25} = \frac{6}{30}$

$\frac{2}{5} = \frac{4}{10} = \frac{6}{15} = \frac{8}{20} = \frac{10}{25} = \frac{12}{30}$

$\frac{3}{5} = \frac{6}{10} = \frac{9}{15} = \frac{12}{20} = \frac{15}{25} = \frac{18}{30}$

$\frac{4}{5} = \frac{8}{10} = \frac{12}{15} = \frac{16}{20} = \frac{20}{25} = \frac{24}{30}$

$\frac{1}{6} = \frac{2}{12} = \frac{3}{18} = \frac{4}{24} = \frac{5}{30}$

$\frac{5}{6} = \frac{10}{12} = \frac{15}{18} = \frac{20}{24} = \frac{25}{30}$

$\frac{1}{7} = \frac{2}{14} = \frac{3}{21} = \frac{4}{28}$

$\frac{2}{7} = \frac{4}{14} = \frac{6}{21} = \frac{8}{28}$

$\frac{3}{7} = \frac{6}{14} = \frac{9}{21} = \frac{12}{28}$

$\frac{4}{7} = \frac{8}{14} = \frac{12}{21} = \frac{16}{28}$

$\frac{5}{7} = \frac{10}{14} = \frac{15}{21} = \frac{20}{28}$

$\frac{6}{7} = \frac{12}{14} = \frac{18}{21} = \frac{24}{28}$

$\frac{1}{8} = \frac{2}{16} = \frac{3}{24}$ $\frac{3}{8} = \frac{6}{16} = \frac{9}{24}$ $\frac{5}{8} = \frac{10}{16} = \frac{15}{24}$ $\frac{7}{8} = \frac{14}{16} = \frac{21}{24}$

$\frac{1}{9} = \frac{2}{18} = \frac{3}{27}$ $\frac{2}{9} = \frac{4}{18} = \frac{6}{27}$ $\frac{4}{9} = \frac{8}{18} = \frac{12}{27}$ $\frac{5}{9} = \frac{10}{18} = \frac{15}{27}$ $\frac{7}{9} = \frac{14}{18} = \frac{21}{27}$ $\frac{8}{9} = \frac{16}{18} = \frac{24}{27}$

$\frac{1}{10} = \frac{2}{20} = \frac{3}{30}$ $\frac{3}{10} = \frac{6}{20} = \frac{9}{30}$ $\frac{7}{10} = \frac{14}{20} = \frac{21}{30}$ $\frac{9}{10} = \frac{18}{20} = \frac{27}{30}$

$\frac{1}{11} = \frac{2}{22}$ $\frac{2}{11} = \frac{4}{22}$ $\frac{3}{11} = \frac{6}{22}$ $\frac{4}{11} = \frac{8}{22}$ $\frac{5}{11} = \frac{10}{22}$ $\frac{6}{11} = \frac{12}{22}$ $\frac{7}{11} = \frac{14}{22}$ $\frac{8}{11} = \frac{16}{22}$ $\frac{9}{11} = \frac{18}{22}$ $\frac{10}{11} = \frac{20}{22}$

$\frac{1}{12} = \frac{2}{24}$ $\frac{5}{12} = \frac{10}{24}$ $\frac{7}{12} = \frac{14}{24}$ $\frac{11}{12} = \frac{22}{24}$

$\frac{1}{13} = \frac{2}{26}$ $\frac{2}{13} = \frac{4}{26}$ $\frac{3}{13} = \frac{6}{26}$ $\frac{4}{13} = \frac{8}{26}$ $\frac{5}{13} = \frac{10}{26}$ $\frac{6}{13} = \frac{12}{26}$ $\frac{7}{13} = \frac{14}{26}$ $\frac{8}{13} = \frac{16}{26}$ $\frac{9}{13} = \frac{18}{26}$ $\frac{10}{13} = \frac{20}{26}$ $\frac{11}{13} = \frac{22}{26}$ $\frac{12}{13} = \frac{24}{26}$

$\frac{1}{14} = \frac{2}{28}$ $\frac{3}{14} = \frac{6}{28}$ $\frac{5}{14} = \frac{10}{28}$ $\frac{9}{14} = \frac{18}{28}$ $\frac{11}{14} = \frac{22}{28}$ $\frac{13}{14} = \frac{26}{28}$

$\frac{1}{15} = \frac{2}{30}$ $\frac{2}{15} = \frac{4}{30}$ $\frac{4}{15} = \frac{8}{30}$ $\frac{7}{15} = \frac{14}{30}$ $\frac{8}{15} = \frac{16}{30}$ $\frac{11}{15} = \frac{22}{30}$ $\frac{13}{15} = \frac{26}{30}$ $\frac{14}{15} = \frac{28}{30}$

Mission File 3:1

Safe and sound

Primary Framework Strands
- Using and applying mathematics

Teaching Content
- Combinations
- Number pattern
- Prediction

Teacher's Notes

Ask children to describe ways of making sure that they have found all combinations of the digits, encouraging a systematic approach.

When questions ask children to make choices, encourage them to include reasons in their answers, not just which safe to select.

Talk about the patterns in the results. Do they recognise the square numbers? Encourage children to use patterns to predict the results before finding all the combinations. Children should use pattern rather than trial and error to solve the Da Vinci files.

TM

1 The Double-3 safe has 9 possible combinations:

11	12	13
21	22	23
31	32	33

2 The 3-Switch safe has 8 possible combinations:

111		
211	121	112
221	212	122
222		

3 Accept a well-reasoned decision. Some children will choose the Double-3 safe as it has more combinations but some children may argue that the 3-Switch is harder to crack as it is not as easy to be sure that you have tried all the combinations.

MM

1 The Double-2 safe has 4 possible combinations:

11	12
21	22

The Double-4 safe has 16 possible combinations:

11	12	13	14
21	22	23	24
31	32	33	34
41	42	43	44

2 The fully completed table is:

Safe	Double-1	Double-2	Double-3	Double-4	Double-5
Number of knobs	2	2	2	2	2
Number of settings	1	2	3	4	5
Number of combinations	1	4	9	16	25

3 There are 25 combinations for the Double-5 safe. Patterns might include the fact that the numbers are square numbers, the difference between them is the odd numbers, the difference increases by 2 each time.

4 The 4-Switch safe has 16 possible combinations:

```
                        1111
          2111  1211  1121  1112
    2211  2121  2112  1221  1212  1122
          2221  2212  2122  1222
                        2222
```

5 The fully completed table is:

Safe	1-Switch	2-Switch	3-Switch	4-Switch	5-Switch
Number of knobs	1	2	3	4	5
Number of settings	2	2	2	2	2
Number of combinations	2	4	8	16	32

6 The 5-Switch safe has 32 possible combinations. The number of combinations doubles each time.

Da Vinci files

A Double-6 safe with 2 knobs, each with 6 settings.

A 7-Switch safe with 7 knobs, each with 2 settings.

Mission File 3:2
Victor's block shocker

Primary Framework Strands
- Using and applying mathematics
- Knowing and using number facts
- Understanding shape

Teaching Content
- Area
- Prime numbers
- Square numbers
- Factors

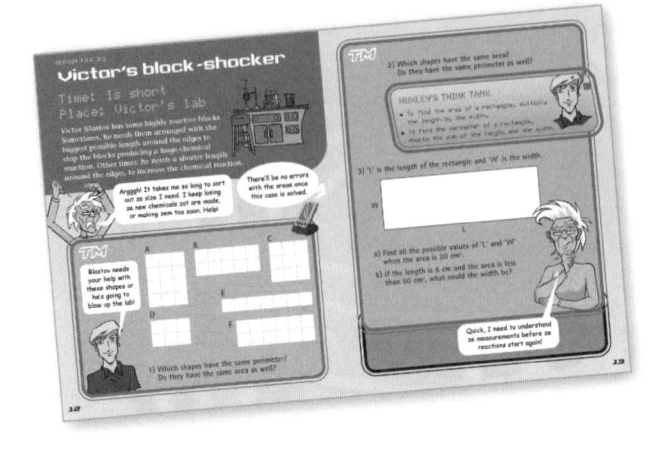

Teacher's Notes

Working from familiar methods of calculating area and extending into area formula, this mission gives children the opportunity to use shape as a visual resource for number facts.

The terms used are clearly defined. As the terms are introduced in the mission, ask children to explain in their own words any terms, which are new to them, to check their understanding.

Encourage children to draw the rectangles as proof of their answers.

TM

1. A and B have the same perimeter (14 cm) but different areas (A = 12 cm^2, B = 10 cm^2).
   E and F have the same perimeter (16 cm) but different areas (E = 7 cm^2, F = 12 cm^2).

2. A and F have the same area (12 cm^2) but different perimeters (A = 14 cm and F = 16 cm).

3. a)

Length	1	2	4	5	10	20
Width	20	10	5	4	2	1

b) 1 cm, 2 cm, 3 cm, 4 cm, 5 cm, 6 cm, 7 cm, 8 cm (allow any values 0.1 to 8.3)

MM

1. a)

Area	2	3	5	7	11	13	17	19	23	29
Rectangle	1 x 2	1 x 3	1 x 5	1 x 7	1 x 11	1 x 13	1 x 17	1 x 19	1 x 23	1 x 29

b) They all have 1 side that has a length of 1 cm.

c) 31 and 37

Supermaths Book 3

2 a) 1, 4, 9, 16, 25

b) The rectangles/shapes they make are squares.

3 area 16, factors 1, 2, 4, 8, 16   rectangles: 1 x 16, 2 x 8, 4 x 4
area 18, factors 1, 2, 3, 6, 9, 18   rectangles: 3 x 6, 2 x 9, 1 x 18
area 20, factors 1, 2, 4, 5, 10, 20   rectangles: 4 x 5, 2 x 10, 1 x 20
area 28, factors 1, 2, 4, 7, 14, 28   rectangles: 4 x 7, 2 x 14, 1 x 28

Da Vinci Files

The numbers less than 30 with 3 factors are all square numbers.
4 – factors 1, 2, 4
9 – factors 1, 3, 9
25 – factors 1, 5, 25

Numbers less than 30 with 4 factors:
6 – factors 1, 2, 3, 6
8 – factors 1, 2, 4, 8
10 – factors 1, 2, 5, 10
14 – factors 1, 2, 7, 14
15 – factors 1, 3, 5, 15
21 – factors 1, 3, 7, 21
22 – factors 1, 2, 11, 22
26 – factors 1, 2, 13, 26
27 – factors 1, 3, 9, 27

Numbers less than 50 with 8 factors:
24 – factors 1, 2, 3, 4, 6, 8, 12, 24
30 – factors 1, 2, 3, 5, 6, 10, 15, 30
40 – factors 1, 2, 4, 5, 8, 10, 20, 40
42 – factors 1, 2, 3, 6, 7, 14, 21, 42

Mission File 3:3
On yer bike

Primary Framework Strands
- Using and applying mathematics
- Counting and understanding number

Teaching Content
- Permutations
- Patterns

Teacher's Notes

This mission gives children the opportunity to work at permutations with a slightly different twist. Most pupils are familiar with bicycles. Ensure that they use the diagrams and text to find information about the other types of cycles, such as unicycles and tricycles.

Allow the children to develop their own methods of working out all the possible solutions, giving credit to children who devise a systematic approach. You may wish to guide children who do not find a working structure by half way through the mission.

TM

1 10

2

Bicycles	0	1	2	3	4
Unicycles	8	6	4	2	0

3

Bicycles	6	5	4	3	2	1	0
Unicycles	1	3	5	7	9	11	13

4

Rider 1	Rider 2	Rider 3	Rider 4	Number of wheels
Unicycle	Unicycle	Unicycle	Unicycle	4
Unicycle	Unicycle	Unicycle	Bicycle	5
Unicycle	Unicycle	Bicycle	Bicycle	6
Unicycle	Bicycle	Bicycle	Bicycle	7
Bicycle	Bicycle	Bicycle	Bicycle	8

5

Bicycles	0	1	2	3	4	5	6
Unicycles	6	5	4	3	2	1	0
Number of wheels	6	7	8	9	10	11	12

Prince Barrington has 4 bicycles and 1 unicycle.

MM

1 a) Teams of 8 people

Types of cycle used	Number of wheels
3 tricycles, 1 bicycle, 1 unicycle	12
2 tricycles, 3 bicycles, 1 unicycle	13
2 tricycles, 2 bicycles, 2 unicycles	12
2 tricycles, 1 bicycle, 3 unicycles	11
1 tricycle, 5 bicycles, 1 unicycle	14
1 tricycle, 4 bicycles, 2 unicycles	12
1 tricycle, 3 bicycles, 3 unicycles	12
1 tricycle, 2 bicycles, 4 unicycles	11
1 tricycle, 1 bicycle, 5 unicycles	10

b) maximum 14, minimum 10

44 Supermaths Book 3

2 a) Teams of 7 people

Types of cycle used	Number of wheels
2 tricycles, 2 bicycles, 1 unicycle	11
2 tricycles, 1 bicycle, 2 unicycles	10
1 tricycle, 4 bicycles, 1 unicycle	12
1 tricycle, 3 bicycles, 2 unicycles	11
1 tricycle, 2 bicycles, 3 unicycles	10
1 tricycle, 1 bicycle, 4 unicycles	9

b) maximum 12, minimum 9

3 a) maximum 10, minimum 8

b) maximum 8, minimum 7

c) maximum 6, minimum 6

Number in the team	Maximum number of wheels	Minimum number of wheels
4	6	6
5	8	7
6	10	8
7	12	9
8	14	10

Maximum number of wheels: increases by 2 as the team increases by 1
  (2 × number in team) − 2
  2 (number in team − 1)

Minimum number of wheels: increases by 1 as the team increases by 1
  number in team + 2

4 maximum 28, minimum 17

Da Vinci files

Number in team	Quads (4 wheels)	Tricycles (3 wheels)	Bicycles (2 wheels)	Unicycles (1 wheel)	Number of wheels	Maximum wheels	Minimum wheels
5	1	1	1	1	10	10	10
6	2	1	1	1	14	14	11
	1	1	2	1	12		
	1	1	1	2	11		
7	3	1	1	1	18	18	12
	2	1	2	1	16		
	2	1	1	2	15		
	1	2	1	1	13		
	1	1	3	1	14		
	1	1	2	2	13		
	1	1	1	3	12		
8	4	1	1	1	22	22	13
	3	1	2	1	20		
	3	1	1	2	19		
	2	2	1	1	18		
	2	1	3	1	18		
	2	1	2	2	17		
	2	1	1	3	16		
	1	2	2	1	15		
	1	2	1	2	14		
	1	1	4	1	16		
	1	1	3	2	15		
	1	1	2	3	14		
	1	1	1	4	13		

Maximum number of wheels: increases by 4 as the team increases by 1
  (4 × number in team) − 10

Minimum number of wheels: increases by 1 as the team increases by 1
  number in team + 5

Mission File 3:4
Make the connection

Primary Framework Strands
- Using and applying mathematics

Teaching Content
- Spatial awareness
- Position
- Patterns

Teacher's Notes

This mission helps to develop good visual and spatial awareness. Some children may prefer to solve it using paper and pen methods. Others may choose to use equipment to solve each part of the puzzle and then record their answers.

Children should use their pattern to solve the questions at the end of the MM – using equipment would be very difficult with the high numbers involved.

An educated guess refined by trial and error is probably the best method for the Da Vinci files.

TM

1 a) 3 rods, 3 connections b) 4 rods, 4 connections c) 4 rods, 3 connections
   d) 4 rods, 5 connections e) 4 rods, 5 connections f) 5 rods, 6 connections
   g) 4 rods, 4 connections h) 6 rods, 10 connections

2 The arrangements of rods in these answers are examples only – it is possible to achieve the same number of connections with other arrangements.

a)  b)  c) d) 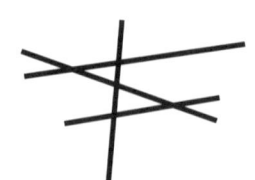 e)  f)

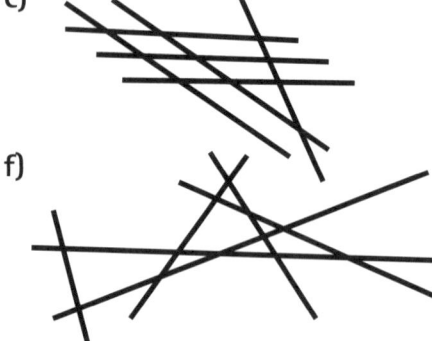

MM

1 The arrangements of rods in these answers are examples only – it is possible to achieve the same number of connections with other arrangements.

2 rods

Number of connections	0	1
Arrangement of rods		

Supermaths Book 3

2 a) 3 rods

Number of connections	0	1	2	3
Arrangement of rods				

b) 4 rods

Number of connections	0	1	2	3	4	5	6
Arrangement of rods							

c) 5 rods

Number of connections	0	1	2	3	4	5	6
Arrangement of rods							

Number of connections	7	8	9	10
Arrangement of rods				

Key points for having found all possible answers are that the connections for each set of rods increase in 1s from 0 to the maximum. For example, 4 rods can have 0, 1, 2, 3, 4, 5 or 6 connections. The absence of a pattern for the maximum number of connections could indicate that some solutions were missed.

3 a)

No of rods	0	1	2	3
Maximum connections	1	3	6	10

Differences + 2   + 3   + 4

Explanation along these lines: the maximum numbers make a pattern, which starts with 1 and has a difference of 2 between the first 2 terms. The differences between the terms increases by 1 for every additional rod.

b) triangular numbers

c) 8 rods would be the 8th triangular number = 36 (1, 3, 6, 10, 15, 21, 28, 36)

d) 10 rods

e) 17 rods

Da Vinci files

12 rods

Answers will vary. This is one possible solution.

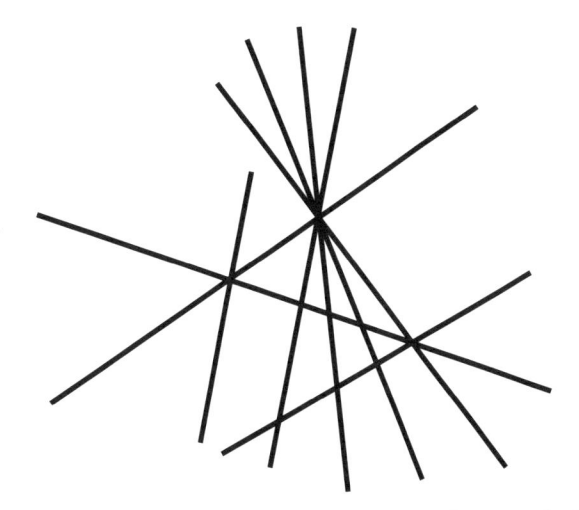

Brain Academy Supermaths Teacher's Book   **47**

Mission File 3:5

What's going on?

Primary Framework Strands
- Using and applying mathematics

Teaching Content
- Logic problems
- Organising and interpreting data

Teacher's Notes

Logic problems are an excellent way to develop systemic working in mathematics problems. This mission would benefit from a logical approach with a clear list of options for each character in each problem. Guide the children, but allow them to experiment with different ways of collating the information.

Children who quickly develop the skills necessary to solve these problems can be encouraged to have 3 or 4 attributes for each character when they create their own puzzle.

Children who take delight in solving these problems would benefit from working through similar problems available in many commercially produced puzzle books.

TM

1 Katy is wearing red, Lisa is wearing blue and Sally is wearing green.

2 John has a miniature recording machine, David has a spy camera and Clare has a walkie-talkie.

3 Tom came by aeroplane on Tuesday, Ann came by train on Monday and Liz came by car on Wednesday.

MM

1 Paul has blue eyes and short, blonde hair.
John has brown eyes and long, brown hair.
Mary has green eyes and long, black hair.

2 Prince Barrington has vanilla ice cream and fruit sauce at 2 p.m.
Sandy has strawberry ice cream and toffee sauce at 10 a.m.
Huxley has chocolate ice cream and a flake after dinner.

3 There are many possible answers. This is one example:
    Prince Barrington had a pizza, but not for dinner.
    Huxley had chips for supper.
    The salad went with the pasta.
    Sandy had her meal at dinnertime.

Da Vinci files

Answers will vary but here is one example of a logic puzzle based on the solution given.
John owns a green vehicle with more than 2 wheels. The bus is blue. A man owns the bike.

Mission File 3:6

The data is later

Primary Framework Strands
- Using and applying mathematics
- Handling data

Teaching Content
- Venn diagrams
- Carroll diagrams
- Patterns

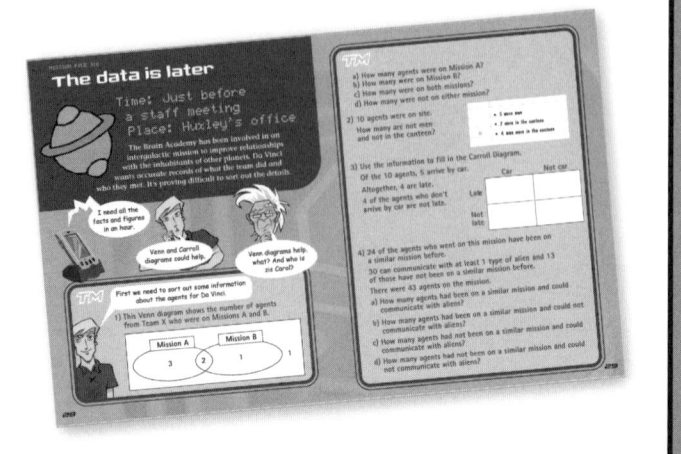

Teacher's Notes

Some of the problems in this mission can be tricky if children try to solve them without using Venn or Carroll diagrams. Once they understand the principles the answers can be easier to deduce. Some children may find this straightforward whilst others may tie themselves in knots – be prepared for both!

The Da Vinci files utilise the skills from the mission in a more extended investigation, with children searching for a pattern that links the results.

TM

1 a) 5 b) 3 c) 2 d) 1

2 2

3

	Car	Not car
Late	3	1
Not late	2	4

4 a) 17 b) 7 c) 13 d) 6

MM

1 5

2 5

3 a) The Venn diagram shows:

4 aliens speak Flibos and travelled 5 light years but are not VIPs.

10 speak Flibos, travelled 5 light years and are VIPs.

2 don't speak Flibos, didn't travel for 5 light years and are not VIPs.

b)

[Venn diagram with three overlapping circles labelled "Speak Flibos", "VIPs", and "Travelled 5 light years". Values: Speak Flibos only = 4; Speak Flibos ∩ VIPs only = 2; VIPs only = 6; Speak Flibos ∩ Travelled only = 3; all three = 10; VIPs ∩ Travelled only = 4; Speak Flibos outside = 2; Travelled only = 7.]

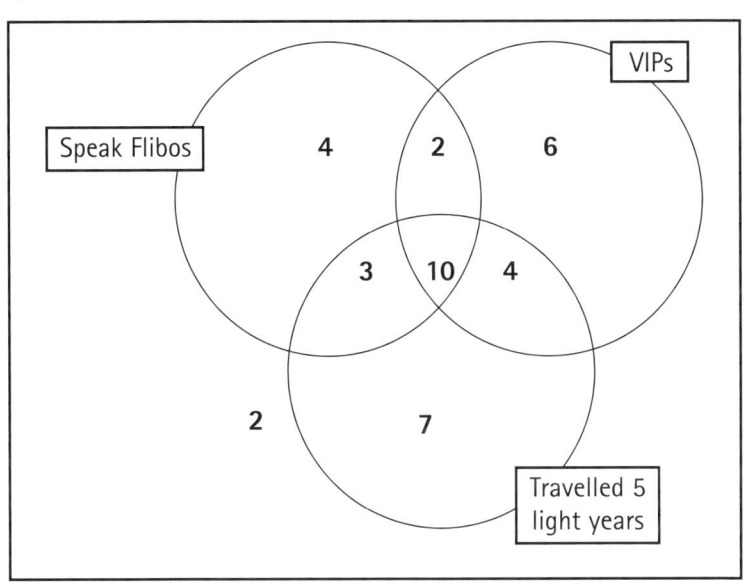

Da Vinci files

Number with cone shape AND wings	0	1	2	3	4	5
Total number of spaceships	11	10	9	8	7	6

Number with cone shape AND wings	0	1	2	3
Total number of spaceships	11	10	9	8

The total number of spaceships with a cone shape **and** wings should equal the maximum number of spaceships.

The greater number of spaceships with a cone shape **or** wings should equal the minimum number of spaceships.

The number of solutions should be 1 greater than the minimum number of spaceships.

Mission File 3:7

When is a Gruffle not a Gruffle?

Primary Framework Strands
- Using and applying mathematics
- Understanding shape

Teaching Content
- Classifying shapes

Teacher's Notes

You might want to start this by doing some 'has/has not' sorting with the children, to ensure that they are just looking at whether something has the property or not.

In the MM, the names and shapes are unfamiliar. The children would benefit from discussing the features that they notice about the shapes. They might come to different conclusions about what makes a Gruffle or a Glimpian. These differences of opinion need discussing.

The children could swap their Glogs from the Da Vinci files, then see if they can define each other's shapes.

Equipment: *cube, triangular prism, square-based pyramid, cuboid*

TM

1 B and C

2 A and D

3 A, C and D

4 answers will vary

MM

1 C and E are definitely Gruffles as they have smooth, curved outlines and 2 blobs inside.

There may well be some debate about F, which could be a Gruffle that happens to be near an extra round blob. Some children might say that it is not a Gruffle as there are 3 small blobs.

2 Make sure that the children's Gruffle matches the agreed definition.

3 B and D are definitely Glimpians. There may be some debate about E, which could be a Glimpian or not, as there are at least 2 possible ways of defining a Glimpian from the evidence supplied:

i) a Glimpian has 2 straight-sided shapes and 1 curved shape. The number of sides of the straight-sided shapes totals 8;

ii) a Glimpian has 3 shapes altogether and the straight-sided shapes have a total of 8 sides. Children may come up with other definitions. If they do, listen to them carefully and test them against the shapes that are given.

4 Make sure that the children's Glimpians match the agreed definition.

Da Vinci Files

Check that the children's creatures are correct for their definitions.

Mission File 3:8
Bazza takes stock...

Primary Framework Strands
- Using and applying mathematics
- Knowing and using number facts
- Understanding shape

Teaching Content
- Multiplication, division and factors
- Cuboids, cubes

Teacher's Notes

Encourage children to find ways of recording the possible arrangements in such a way that they can find them all without including repeats. You will need to agree whether to call it a repeat when you have the same arrangement with the box 'standing up' or 'lying down'. The answers include both, but you might decide not to. Some children might want to draw the shapes, in which case isometric dotty paper (triangular dotted paper) could be useful.

For MM questions 2) and 3), talk about practical considerations such as fitting boxes in cupboards, the strength of the boxes and so on. An interesting spin off is to consider how much card each arrangement would take, maybe using 2 cm paper and interlocking cubes to help. Which box for 18 uses the least amount of card?

Equipment: *interlocking cubes, squared paper, isometric dotty paper*

1 The possible arrangements for 12 cubes, including repeats where the box is either 'standing up' or 'lying down' are:

Number per layer	Arranged as	Height
1	1 × 1	12
2	1 × 1	6
3	1 × 3	4
4	1 × 4	3
4	2 × 2	3
6	1 × 6	2
6	2 × 3	2
12	1 × 12	1
12	2 × 6	1
12	3 × 4	1

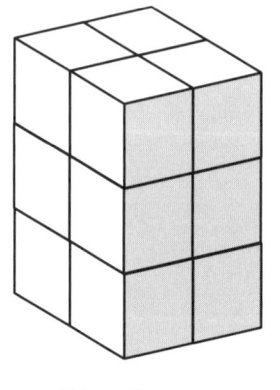

Standing up 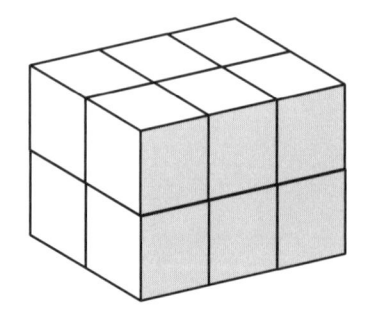   Lying down

54   Supermaths Book 3

MM

1 The possible arrangements for 18 cubes, including repeats where the box is either 'standing up' or 'lying down', are:

Number per layer	Arranged as	Height
1	1 × 1	18
2	1 × 1	9
3	1 × 3	6
6	1 × 6	3
6	2 × 3	3
9	1 × 9	2
9	3 × 3	2
18	1 × 18	1
18	2 × 9	1
18	3 × 6	1

2 and **3**

Hear the children's ideas and reasons. Generally, long thin boxes are not as strong as boxes that are closer to a cube shape. Nor do they pack on shelves quite as easily.

If you wanted to develop this work, you could try making some of the boxes and comparing their surface areas. (Making the boxes from 2-cm squared paper is useful for this and matches the size of common interlocking cubes.) A manufacturer would consider the amount of card needed for each box when working out costs.

4 a) 6

b) 4

c) 3 small + 4 medium or 6 small + 2 medium

d) 3 medium + 2 large

e) 3 small + 1 medium + 2 large

5 a) no   **b)** no   **c)** n

The closest to 100 they can get whilst still having 100 cubes is 102.

There are 3 ways of doing this:
1 large + 7 medium
3 large + 4 medium
5 large + 1 medium

It might be interesting to look at the pattern in these results when they are written in order, noting how as the number of large boxes increases by 2 the number of medium boxes decreases by 3. Why is this? Would something similar happen with other totals?

The smallest number of boxes they can use is 6. This could be 6 large or 5 large + 1 medium.

Da Vinci files

The next 2 sizes of cube-shaped boxes will hold 27 and 64 cubes.

512 cubes in an 8 × 8 × 8 cube that has 8 layers of 64

Mission File 3:9
Cycle paths

Primary Framework Strands
- Using and applying mathematics

Teaching Content
- Networks
- Reasoning

Teacher's Notes

You might want to start with the old 'house' or 'open envelope' puzzle – can you draw this shape without lifting your pencil off the paper or going over any line twice?

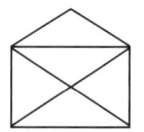

Networks that you can draw in this way are called traversable. A traversable network will either have no junctions with an odd number of roads (an odd junction), or just 2 junctions with an odd number of roads. They can have as many even junctions as they like. This leads to a nice opportunity for reasoned proof. To start this, you might like to challenge the children to draw a network with an odd number of odd junctions and, after a while, ask them why it is impossible. It can be interesting to ask them to draw a route with just 1 odd junction.

Apart from the start and finish towns, all other towns need roads in pairs so that you can get in to them and go out of them again, so these 'pass through' towns must have even junctions. The start and finish towns can have odd junctions as you are not just passing through them. As you can't have more than 1 start or more than 1 finish, you can't have more than 2 odd junctions.

TM

All roads can be travelled along just once for routes 1, 2 and 3. It is not possible for route 4.

MM

1 All roads can be travelled along just once for routes a and b. It is not possible for routes c and d.

2 a) [network diagram with nodes A(2), B(2), C(3), D(3)]
   b) [network diagram with nodes A(2), B(3), C(3), D(2)]

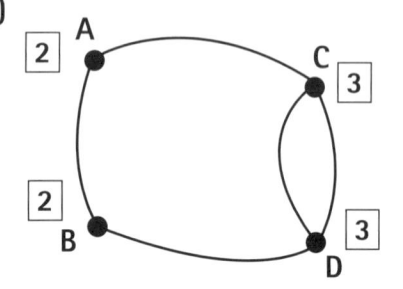

56 Supermaths Book 3

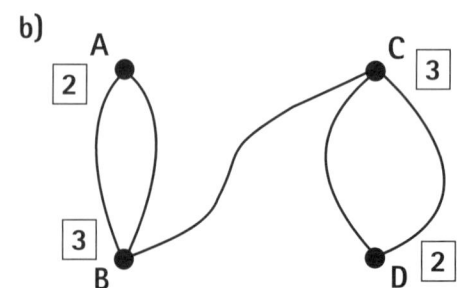

c)

d)

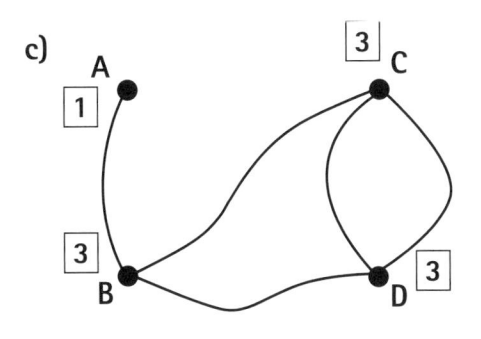

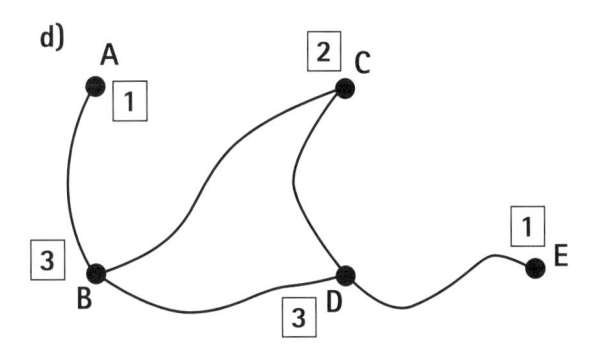

3 2

4 4

5 You start and finish at a town with an odd number of roads. You are passing through all other towns, so you need roads in pairs to get in and go out, so the towns you pass through between the start and finish must have an even number of roads. That is why you cannot have more than 2 towns with an odd number of roads if you are going to use all the roads.

Before telling the children this, you might want them to draw their own routes and explore what happens for themselves. It can be interesting to ask them to draw a route with just one odd town!

Da Vinci files

1 The largest number of roads you can travel along without using any road twice is 13. There are several ways of doing this. One way is shown.

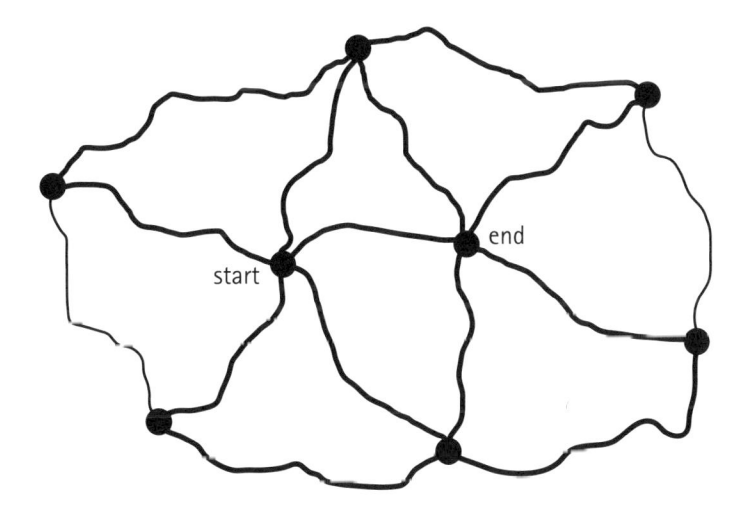

Mission File 4:1

Hose in the house?

Primary Framework Strands
- Calculating

Teaching Content
- Calculation with length and money

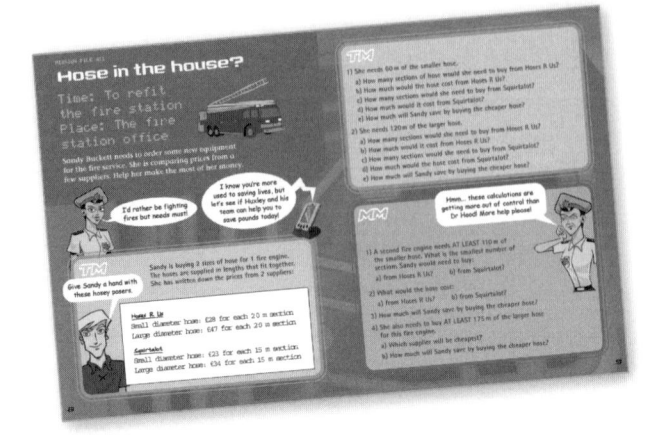

Teacher's Notes

Ask children to explain how they worked out how many sections that they need from each supplier. They may well use informal methods of division based on multiplication and maybe doubling.

In MM question 4), the exact lengths cannot be made using a whole number of sections. Make sure that the children realise that they need to buy more than the required length in order to have at least enough hose.

With the ladders, some children might think that the number of spaces between the rungs is the same as the number of rungs. Encourage them to try a few examples for themselves to see that this is not the case.

TM

1 a) 3   b) £84   c) 4   d) £92   e) £8

2 a) 6   b) £282   c) 8   d) £272   e) £10

Did the children spot that the number of sections would be twice the number needed for the 60 m length in question 1?

MM

1 a) 6   b) 8

2 a) £168   b) £184

3 £16

4 a) Squirtalot   b) £15

5 a) £354 (11 × 20 + 2 × 15)

   b) £378 (2 × 20 + 14 × 15)

6 £795 (1 × 20 + 22 × 15)

58   Supermaths Book 4

7 a) 3 m 50 cm   **b)** 16 rungs

8 a) Children's explanation should include the fact that there are 6 rungs that cost £2.80 each and that 6 × £2.80 = £16.80

b) There are five 30 cm 'spaces' between the rungs and two 25 cm 'spaces' at the ends, so the ladder is 2 m long. Each side costs 2 × £1.25 and there are 2 sides, so they cost 2 × 2 × £1.25 or 4 × £1.25

c) £21.80

9 £92.80 (£72.80 for the rungs, £20 for the sides)

Da Vinci files

$13 \frac{1}{2}$ minutes

20 litres per second

1 minute $7 \frac{1}{2}$ seconds

Mission File 4:2

Happy birthday, Victor!

Primary Framework Strands
- Counting and understanding number

Teaching Content
- Addition
- Place value

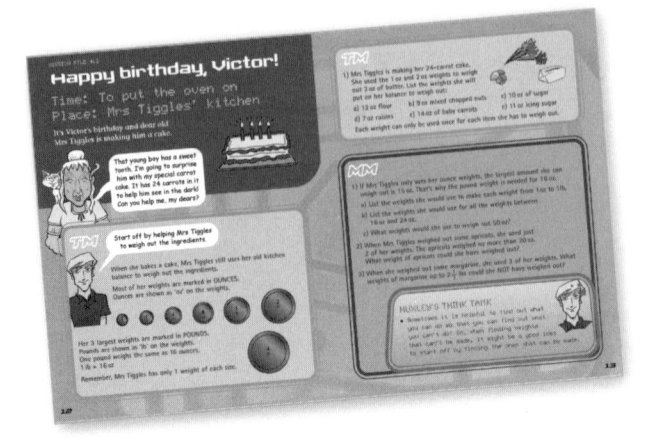

Teacher's Notes

Both the examples used in this mission use the base 2 number system where the column headings are units, 2s, 4s, 8s, 16s and so on, exchanging at 2 rather than the more familiar 10.

The first example is an old application, where the weights for a set of kitchen balances are 1, 2, 4, 8 and 16 oz, which were originally chosen for the very good reason that just 1 of each weight was all that is needed to make all the possible values. This is more efficient than having, say, a 1 g, 5 g, 10 g set where you need at least 4 of the 1 g weights to get all the weights from 1 g to 19 g.

The second application is an old version of a current use of base 2, which is in computers where switches can either be on or off (or 1 as you often see marked on on/off switches these days). The paper tape example is very visual. ASCII code is still used to represent letters.

Help children make the links between both examples.

TM

1 a) 8 oz + 4 oz   b) 8 oz + 1 oz   c) 8 oz + 2 oz
   d) 4 oz + 2 oz + 1 oz   e) 8 oz + 4 oz + 2 oz   f) 8 oz + 2 oz + 1 oz

MM

1) a) 1 oz, 2 oz, 2 oz + 1 oz, 4 oz, 4 oz + 1 oz, 4 oz + 2 oz, 4 oz + 2 oz + 1 oz,
      8 oz, 8 oz + 1oz, 8 oz + 2 oz, 8 oz + 2 oz + 1 oz, 8 oz + 4 oz, 8 oz + 4 oz + 1 oz,
      8 oz + 4 oz + 2 oz, 8 oz + 4 oz + 2 oz + 1 oz, 1lb

   b) 1 lb, 1 lb + 1 oz, 1 lb + 2 oz, 1 lb + 2 oz + 1 oz, 1 lb + 4 oz, 1 lb + 4 oz + 1 oz,
      1 lb + 4 oz + 2 oz, 1 lb + 4 oz + 2 oz + 1 oz, 1 lb + 8 oz

   c) 2 lb + 1 lb + 2 oz

2 3 oz, 5 oz, 6 oz, 9 oz, 10 oz, 12 oz, 17 oz, 18 oz, 20 oz

3 1 oz, 2 oz, 3 oz, 4 oz, 5 oz, 6 oz, 8 oz, 9 oz, 10 oz, 12 oz, 15 oz, 16 oz, 17 oz, 18 oz,
   20 oz, 23 oz, 24 oz, 27 oz, 29 oz, 30 oz, 31 oz, 32 oz, 33 oz, 34 oz, 36 oz, 39 oz, 40 oz

4 a) 90   **b)** 4 lb + 1 lb + 8 oz + 2 oz

5 a) 101   **b)** 4 lb + 2 lb + 4 oz + 1 oz

6 a) 45   **b)** 2 lb + 8 oz + 4 oz + 1 oz

7 a) b) c) d) e) f)

8 Reading downwards, the numbers are 99, 97, 107 and 101 which represent c, a, k and e.

9 apple

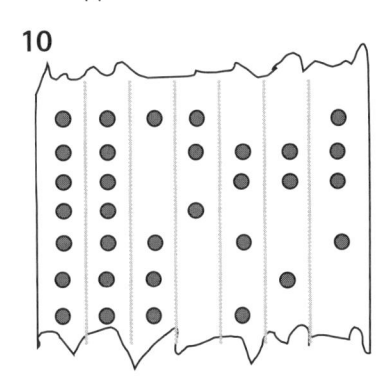

10

Da Vinci files

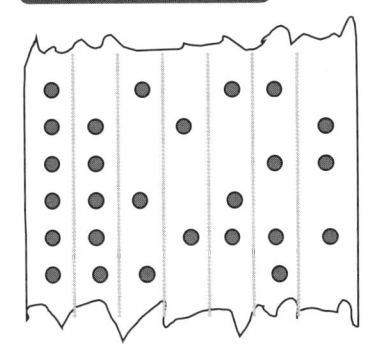

the capital letter X

Mission File 4:3

A sticker situation for Tex

Primary Framework Strands
- Knowing and using number facts

Teaching Content
- Multiples
- Common multiples
- Reasoning

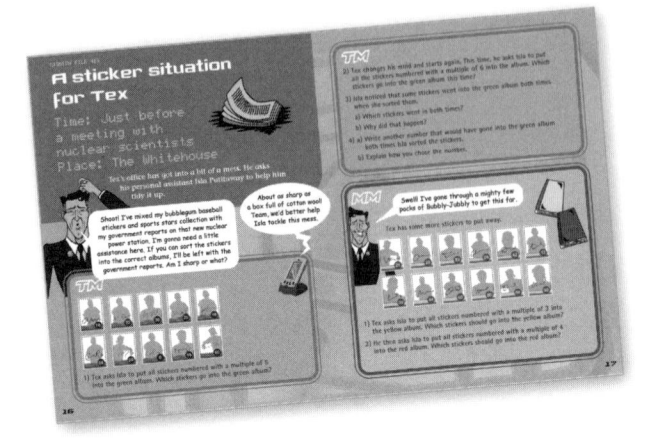

Teacher's Notes

Make sure that children understand the term multiple.

You might need to try a few examples with the tests of divisibility given in Huxley's Think Tank to make sure that the children understand them.

When arranging numbers so that there are no common multiples (other than multiples of 1) next to each other, it might help some children if they listed what each number was a multiple of (the factors of the number excluding 1). Some children might find it helpful to do this on scraps of paper so that they can move the numbers around.

The Da Vinci files can be worked without listing all the numbers. See the answers for more details.

TM

1 15, 25, 30, 60

2 6, 18, 24, 30, 60

3 a) 30 and 60   b) They are multiples of both 5 and 6.

4 a) any multiple of 30
   b) Children's explanation – it could be trial and error or they could have chosen a multiple of 3.

MM

1 12, 21, 33, 36, 42, 60, 66, 90

2 12, 20, 28, 36, 44, 60, 80

3 a) 12, 36 and 60
   b) Children's explanation – it should include something about 12, 36 and 60 belonging in both folders and might include that they are multiples of 12.

4 any 3 multiples of 12 other than 12, 36, 48 and 60

Supermaths Book 4

5 a) and **b)** Check that no number is next to another that is a multiple of the same number other than 1.
Here are 2 ways of arranging the numbers – there may be more.

(15)(14)(33)(10)(21)(25)(17)(20)   (10)(17)(15)(14)(25)(21)(20)(33)

6 Check that no number is next to another that is a multiple of the same number other than 1.
Here are 2 ways of arranging the numbers – there may be more.

(48)(47)(39)(25)(28)(27)(35)(24)(61)(90)   (24)(61)(90)(47)(35)(48)(25)(39)(28)(27)

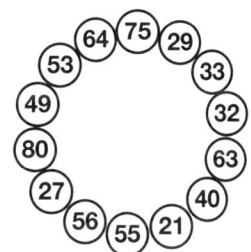

7 Children's own set of numbers. Check that no number is next to another that is a multiple of the same number other than 1.

8 Check that no number is next to another that is a multiple of the same number other than 1.
Here is one way of arranging the numbers – there may be more.

(64)(75)(29)(53)(33)(49)(32)(80)(63)(27)(40)(56)(55)(21)

9 Children's own set of numbers. Check that no number is next to another that is a multiple of the same number other than 1.

Da Vinci files

80 numbers go into the box. There are several ways of tackling this. One would be to work through the numbers 1–200 one at a time, listing the ones that are not multiples of either 2 or 5 and then counting those to find out how many there are.

A more efficient way of doing the same thing would be to use a 1–100 square and shade out all the multiples of 2 and 5 to see how many are left. The same would happen if it was a 101–200 square, so double the number.

However, as the question only asks how many numbers there are in the box and not what the numbers are, the solution could be reached with a bit of division:
  200 ÷ 2 = 100, so there must be 100 multiples of 2 from 1 to 200
  200 ÷ 5 = 40, so there must be 40 multiples of 5
But some multiples of 2 and 5 are also multiples of 10, so these will have been counted twice:
  200 ÷ 10 = 20, so 20 have been counted twice
Altogether there are 100 + 40 − 20 = 120 multiples of either 2 or 5 in the numbers 1 to 200, so there must be 80 numbers in the box that are not multiples of either 2 or 5

Brain Academy Supermaths Teacher's Book

Mission File 4:4
Fractious fractions

Primary Framework Strands
- Calculating

Teaching Content
- Fractions
- Decimals

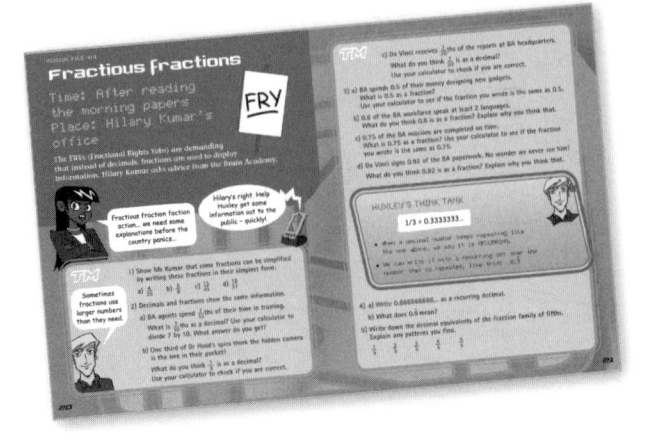

Teacher's Notes

Calculators are required for most of this mission and access to currency exchange rates is required for the final section. While there is an initial check on common fractions and decimals, the focus quickly moves to less well-known decimals. Trial and refinement will probably be the initial strategy for solving, but you may wish to extend the brightest pupils by looking at the rules/patterns for turning recurring decimals into fractions. In brief, these are:

One recurring number is placed over 9, e.g. $0.2222... = \frac{2}{9}$

Two recurring numbers are placed over 99, e.g. $0.272727... = \frac{27}{99} = \frac{3}{11}$

Three recurring numbers are placed over 999, e.g. $0.124124... = \frac{124}{999}$ and so on.

If there are zeros before the repeating number/pattern, then those zeros are placed after the 9s in the denominator, e.g. $0.007777... = \frac{7}{900}$, $0.0002424... = \frac{24}{99000}$

so $0.0769230769... = \frac{769230}{9999990} = \frac{1}{13}$

If there are digits before the recurring pattern starts, the decimal is split into 2 fractions.

e.g. $0.08333... = 0.08 + 0.003333... = \frac{8}{100} + \frac{3}{900} = \frac{75}{900} = \frac{1}{12}$

TM

1 a) $\frac{1}{5}$ b) $\frac{3}{4}$ c) $\frac{1}{3}$ d) $\frac{2}{3}$

2 a) 0.7   b) 0.3333...   c) 0.35

3 a) $\frac{1}{2}$

   b) $\frac{3}{5}$ because 0.6 is six tenths (by place value) and $\frac{6}{10} = \frac{3}{5}$

   c) $\frac{3}{4}$

   d) $\frac{23}{25}$ because 0.92 is 92 hundredths = $\frac{92}{100}$ (accept any equivalent fractions in Q3)

4 a) $0.\dot{6}$ b) 0.9999999... the nine carries on repeating

5 $\frac{1}{5} = 0.2$ $\frac{2}{5} = 0.4$ $\frac{3}{5} = 0.6$ $\frac{4}{5} = 0.8$ $\frac{5}{5} = 1.0$

Explanation, e.g. double the numerator and divide by 10.

Supermaths Book 4

MM

Children need a calculator with a 12-digit display, or they can use a computer to see recurring sequences of 6 digits or more. They could also use a spreadsheet.

1 9

2 a) $\frac{2}{9} = 0.222... = 0.\dot{2}$ **b)** $\frac{3}{9} = 0.333... = 0.\dot{3}$

  c) $\frac{4}{9} = 0.444... = 0.\dot{4}$ **d)** $\frac{5}{9} = 0.555... = 0.\dot{5}$

  e) Up to $\frac{8}{9} = 0.\dot{8}$
  The decimal is always the top digit repeated after the decimal point.

  f) $\frac{10}{9} = 1.\dot{1}$ $\frac{11}{9} = 1.\dot{2}$ $\frac{12}{9} = 1.\dot{3}$

  Explanation, e.g. divide the numerator by 10 and write a recurring dot after it.

  Rule changes: the number before the decimal point is the result of dividing the number by 9 and the recurring digit after the decimal point is the remainder.

3 a) 11

  b) $\frac{2}{11} = 0.181818...$ $\frac{3}{11} = 0.272727...$ $\frac{4}{11} = 0.363636...$ $\frac{5}{11} = 0.454545...$

  $\frac{6}{11} = 0.545454...$ $\frac{7}{11} = 0.636363...$ $\frac{8}{11} = 0.727272...$ $\frac{9}{11} = 0.81818...$

  $\frac{10}{11} = 0.909090....$

  c) Divide the top number (numerator) by 11. The answer goes before the decimal point.
  Multiply the remainder by 9 and that is the repeating pattern after the decimal point.

4 a) $\frac{1}{18}$

  b) $\frac{2}{18} = 0.\dot{1}$ $\frac{3}{18} = 0.16\dot{6}$ $\frac{4}{18} = 0.\dot{2}$ $\frac{5}{18} = 0.27\dot{7}$

  $\frac{6}{18} = 0.\dot{3}$ $\frac{7}{18} = 0.38\dot{8}$ $\frac{8}{18} = 0.\dot{4}$ $\frac{9}{18} = 0.5$

  $\frac{10}{18} = 0.\dot{5}$ $\frac{10}{18} = 0.6\dot{1}$ $\frac{12}{18} = 0.\dot{6}$ $\frac{13}{18} = 0.72\dot{2}$

  $\frac{14}{18} = 0.\dot{7}$ $\frac{15}{18} = 0.83\dot{3}$ $\frac{16}{18} = 0.\dot{8}$ $\frac{17}{18} = 0.94\dot{4}$

  Sample explanation:
  The even numerators follow the pattern of ninths (because they are equivalent to ninths).

  The odd numerators take the digit from the even numerator just before them and use the digit which gives a difference of 5. That digit is recurring.

5 a) 1/7

  b) Answers are given to 12 decimal places to show the repeating pattern.

  $\frac{1}{7} = 0.142857142\ 857$ $\frac{2}{7} = 0.285714285714$ $\frac{3}{7} = 0.428571428571$

  $\frac{4}{7} = 0.571428571428$ $\frac{5}{7} = 0.714285714285$ $\frac{6}{7} = 857142857142$

  Sample explanation: the repeating pattern is the same in each of these, but it starts at different digits in the pattern.

Da Vinci files

Answers will vary. Check the children's answers.

Mission File 4:5

Spot the sausage!

Primary Framework Strands
- Using and applying mathematics

Teaching Content
- Number pattern
- Prediction

Teacher's Notes

Talk about ways of ensuring the maximum number of crossings. For example:
- Each line should cross every other line.
- If you draw 3 lines so that they all cross at the same point, you can increase the number of crossings to 3 by moving 1 of the lines across a little.

Encourage children to look for patterns in the results. Do any of the children spot that the largest number of crossings are the triangle numbers?

Encourage children to use pattern to predict the results, both in and between the crossings and the cuts. They should use these patterns to help solve the Da Vinci files, rather than doing so with drawings or trial and error.

TM

1 20p as you need at least 2 lines to make a crossing

2 He could make 3 crossings.

3 a) More crossings are possible.

b) The greatest number of crossings is 6.

MM

1 The difference in the number of crossings is increasing by 1 each time.

2 a) 10   b) 15

3 Check that the children's drawings show 10 and 15 crossings.

4
Number of lines	Largest number of crossings
1	0
2	1
3	3
4	6
5	10
6	15

5 7

6 11

7
Number of cuts	Largest number of pieces
0	1
1	2
2	4
3	7
4	11

8 a) 16   b) 22   c) Check the children's drawings.

Da Vinci Files

£1 for 10 lines which could give 55 crossings

120 crossings from 15 lines

13 cuts which gives 92 pieces. 12 cuts only gives 79 pieces, which is not enough.

Brain Academy Supermaths Teacher's Book 67

Mission File 4:6

Per cent per chance?

Primary Framework Strands
- Counting and understanding number

Teaching Content
- Calculating
- Percentages

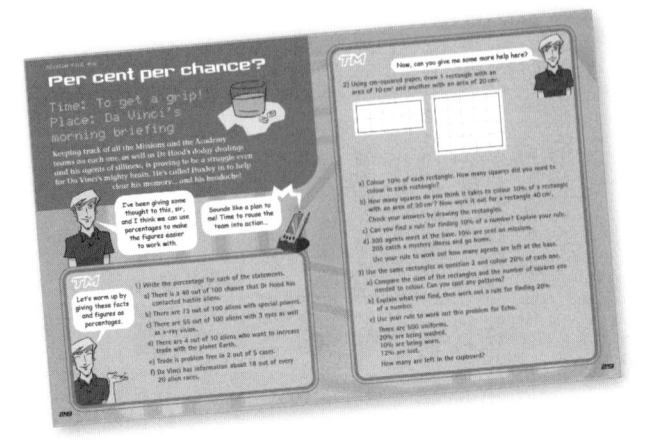

Teacher's Notes

This mission gives children the opportunity to discover quick ways to calculate percentages and then to use the methods they find. After an initial check on the principles of percentage notation, children use a visual stimulus to develop their understanding and to devise rules. Encourage children to draw the rectangles accurately as the visual impact of seeing that a percentage changes with the size of the shape is very valuable.

The rules devised are then tested in contextual but non-visual settings before an investigational challenge at the end.

TM

1 a) 40%   **b)** 73%   **c)** 55%   **d)** 40%   **e)** 40%   **f)** 90%

2 a) 1 in 10 cm² rectangle and 2 in 20 cm² rectangle

   b) 3 in 30 cm² rectangle and 4 in 40 cm² rectangle

   c) divide by 10 to find 10% because 10% is $\frac{1}{10}$

   d) 65

3 a) 10 cm² = 2 squares   20 cm² = 4 squares   30 cm² = 6 squares   40 cm² = 8 squares

   b) divide by 10 and double

   c) 290

Supermaths Book 4

MM

1

Area of rectangle	Number of squares you need to colour to make			
	10%	20%	30%	40%
10 cm²	1	2	3	4
20 cm²	2	4	6	8
30 cm²	3	6	9	12
40 cm²	4	8	12	16
50 cm²	5	10	15	20

To find 10% divide by 10 or divide by 100 and x 10.
To find 20% divide by 10 and x 2 or divide by 100 and x 20.
To find 30% divide by 10 and x 3 or divide by 100 and x 30.
To find 40% divide by 10 and x 4 or divide by 100 and x 40.
To find 50% divide by 10 and x 5 or divide by 100 and x 50 **or** halve the number.

2

Number of agents	Number of agents needed for			
	10%	20%	30%	40%
60 agents	6	12	18	24
70 agents	7	14	21	28
90 agents	9	18	27	36
100 agents	10	20	30	40
300 agents	30	60	90	120

3 Check the children's suggestions, e.g. divide by 10 and multiply by 7.

4 69

5 72

Da Vinci files

Range 200 to 2000 (10% of 200 = 20; 1% of 2000 = 20).

Range 400 if 80% use the visitors' gate to 500 if they all use the visitors' gate.
(80% = 400 so 100% = 500)

Needs number 1 as the number given in the question.

E.g. Maximum of 20% of agents work through the night. If 1 worked through the night, what is the range of number of agents?

Mission File 4:7

The truth is out there...

Primary Framework Strands
- Knowing and using number facts

Teaching Content
- Prime numbers
- Factors
- Prime factors

Teacher's Notes

This mission is great for helping children understand and remember both prime numbers and factors. In the first section, ensure that pupils know and use the fact the prime numbers have 2 (and only 2) factors – the number itself and the number 1. One is not a prime number because it has only 1 factor.

Prime factors make interesting puzzles and this mission gives an excellent grounding for developing this knowledge and work at KS3.

The final challenge may require access to a computer to research the name and use of index numbers. They are a wonderful way to write calculations in shorthand and more able pupils love the 'power' of them.

TM

1 **a)** 2, 3, 5, 7, 11, 13, 17, 19, 23, 29, 31, 37, 41, 43, 47

  b) All the other even numbers are multiples of 2, so they will have at least the factors 1, 2 and themselves and cannot be prime.

2 **a)** 1 ② 4 8

  b) 1 ③ ⑤ 15

  c) 1 ② ③ 4 6 8 12 24

  d) 1 ② ③ ⑤ 6 10 15 30

  e) 1 ㉓

  f) 1 ② ③ 4 6 9 12 18 36

3 **a)** 3×5 **b)** $2 \times 2 \times 2 \times 3$ **c)** $2 \times 3 \times 5$ **d)** $2 \times 2 \times 2 \times 5$ **e)** $3 \times 3 \times 5$ **f)** $3 \times 3 \times 7$

4 **a)** 10 **b)** 30

  c) 21 **d)** 924

  e) 39 **f)** 102

70 Supermaths Book 4

MM

1 no, e.g. 1 × 1 = 1 (because 1 is not a prime number)
2 × 2 × 3 × 3 = 36, 2 × 2 × 5 × 5 = 100

2 2 × 3 × 7 = 42

3 5 numbers from
2 × 3 × 3 × 5 = 60   2 × 3 × 11 = 6
62 × 5 × 7 = 70   2 × 3 × 13 = 78
2 × 2 × 3 × 7 = 84   2 × 3 × 3 × 5 = 90

4 a) 2 × 3 × 5 × 7 = 210   **b)** 2 × 3 × 5 × 7 × 11 = 2310

5 2 × 2 = 4   2 × 2 × 2 = 8
2 × 2 × 2 × 2 = 16   2 × 2 × 2 × 2 × 2 = 32
2 × 2 × 2 × 2 × 2 × 2 = 64   3 × 3 = 9
3 × 3 × 3 = 27   3 × 3 × 3 × 3 = 81
5 × 5 = 25   7 × 7 = 49

Children may also include all the prime numbers less than 100.

Da Vinci files

Five is an index number (plural indices). It tells you how many times to multiply a number by itself.
E.g. 25 = 2 × 2 × 2 × 2 × 2

$90 = 2 \times 3^2 \times 5$ $91 = 7 \times 13$

$92 = 2^2 \times 23$ $93 = 3 \times 31$

$94 = 2 \times 47$ $95 = 5 \times 19$

$96 = 2^5 \times 3$ $97 = 97^1$

$98 = 2 \times 7^2$ $99 = 3^2 \times 11$

$100 = 2^2 \times 5^2$

Mission File 4:8

Rock on, Buster C!

Primary Framework Strands
- Understanding shape

Teaching Content
- Angle sum of triangles
- Angle sum of polygons

Teacher's Notes

This mission reinforces that the fact that the angle sum of every triangle is 180°. It links the angle sum of different polygons with the minimum number of triangles into which each polygon can be divided.

Protractors are not required, as the angle sums are all multiples of 180° (and create straight lines and whole turns when cut and pasted). However, the mission could be supported by the use of protractors if you wished to give the children extra practice in measuring angles.

The final challenge with the sum of external angles could be extended to finding the external angles of regular polygons, which is part of the KS3 curriculum.

TM

1 a) angles can be fitted together to show a straight line

   b) angle sum of triangle = 180°

2 all triangles have angle sum of 180°

3 a) angles fit together to make 2 straight lines

   b) angle sum of rectangle = 360°

4 a) angle sum of all the quadrilaterals = 360°

   b) angle sum of any quadrilateral = 360°

5 always 2 triangles

MM

1 a) angle sum of all pentagons is 540°   b) 3

2 a) angle sum of all hexagons is 720°   b) 4

3 a) angle sum of all heptagons is 900°   b) 5

4 a) angle sum of all octagons is 1080°   b) 6

72 Supermaths Book 4

5 a)

Number of sides	Shape names	Smallest number of triangles you can split the shape into	The angle sum
3	triangle	1	180°
4	quadrilateral	2	360°
5	pentagon	3	540°
6	hexagon	4	720°
7	heptagon	5	900°
8	octagon	6	1,080°

Possible relationships:

i) number sides − 2 = number of triangles

ii) number triangles × 180° = angle sum of shape

iii) angle sum ÷ number of triangles = 180°

iv) (number sides − 2) × 180° = angle sum of shape

b) (10 − 2) × 180° = 1440°

Da Vinci files

The exterior angle sum of the red triangle is 360°.
The external angle sum of any polygon is 360°.

Mission File 4:9

What a clever pussy you are, you are... oh what a clever pussy, you are!

Primary Framework Strands
- Handling data

Teaching Content
- Averages: mean, median, mode
- Range

Teacher's Notes

This mission gives children the opportunity to use different measures of average and reinforces their understanding of them. There is an opportunity for the revision of terms and how to calculate the measures before the more investigative work starts.

For the main block of work, encourage children to draw lines or boxes for the number of terms in each puzzle. The puzzles are easier to solve if the terms are kept in order (smallest to largest is the most logical). If the median is written in first, the position of the mode can be ascertained.

When puzzles give the mean as well, remind children that they need to make sure the terms they choose give the required total. These puzzles are tricky (but fun) to solve and create.

TM

1 The **mode** is a measure of average and is the item that occurs most often in a sample.

The **median** is a measure of average and is the middle number in a set once the numbers have been arranged in order of size.

The **range** is a measure of the spread of the data and is the difference between the highest and lowest values.

The **mean** is a measure of average and is the sum of all the items in a set divided by the number of items.

2 **a)** to **d)**

Data Set	Range	Mode	Median	Mean
A	3	3	3	4
B	4	2 and 5	2	3
C	9	1	2	3
D	6	4	4	5
E	9	10	3.5	5
F	11	3	5	6.5

Supermaths Book 4

e) The mean, median and mode are not exactly the same for any of the given sets. For some sets, like Set A, the 3 values are fairly close. For others, like Set B, 2 values are the same). In some sets, like Set E, there are quite big differences in the values. This is because each measure calculates the average using a different method.

f) The children's answers will vary depending on the relative value of the number they remove from the set. If the number is above the original average, the measure will fall (the larger the number removed, the greater the fall in the measure). If the number is below the original average, the measure will rise (the smaller the number removed, the greater the rise in the measure). If the number is close to the original average, there will be little or no change.

MM

1 a) 3, 3, 8   mean = 3.67

   b) 5, 6, 7, 8, 8   mean = 6.8

   c) 5, 5, 6, 6, 9, 9, 9   mean = 5.57

2 a) 6, 6, 8   (mean = 6.67)
       4, 6, 6   (mean = 5.33)

   b) 3, 3, 5, 6, 10   (mean = 5.4)
       3, 3, 5, 7, 10   (mean = 5.6)
       3, 3, 5, 8, 10   (mean = 5.8)

   c) 0, 5, 5, 5   (mean = 3.75)
       1, 5, 5, 6   (mean = 4.25)
       2, 5, 5, 7   (mean = 4.75)
       3, 5, 5, 8   (mean = 5.25)
       4, 5, 5, 9   (mean = 5.75)
       5, 5, 5, 10   (mean = 6.25)

   d) 7, 8, 8, 10, 11, 13   (mean = 9.5)
       7, 8, 8, 10, 12, 13   (mean = 9.67)
       8, 8, 8, 10, 10, 14   (mean = 9.67)
       8, 8, 8, 10, 11, 14   (mean = 9.83)
       8, 8, 8, 10, 12, 14   (mean = 10)
       8, 8, 8, 10, 13, 14   (mean = 10.17)
       8, 8, 8, 10, 14, 14   (mean = 10.3)

3 a) 1, 1, 3, 7, 8

   b) 2, 4, 5, 7, 9, 9

   c) 0, 0, 2, 7, 8, 8, 10

   d) 1, 1, 1, 5, 5, 7, 8 **and** 1, 1, 1, 5, 6, 6, 8

Da Vinci Files

Check the children's own problems.

Mission File 5:1

Pussy patterns

Primary Framework Strands
- Using and applying mathematics

Teaching Content
- Shape
- Pattern
- Reasoning

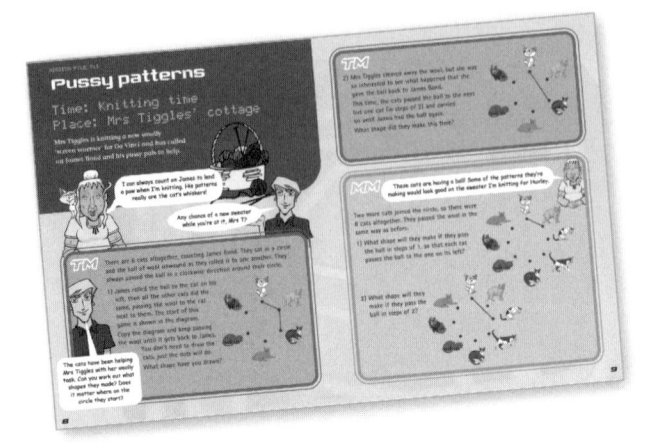

Teacher's Notes

You could start this activity in a practical way with the children passing a ball of wool or string to one another in different steps. If you do, then it would be best to start with a number that isn't used in the mission.

Make sure that the children are familiar with the names of the shapes given in Huxley's Think Tank.

After the children have worked through some examples, encourage them to predict what will happen for given numbers and to think about why certain shapes occur. For example, do they realise that steps of 3 will give a triangle on a 9-dot circle because 9 ÷ 3 = 3, or that a square can be made on a 20-dot circle by using steps of 5 because 20 ÷ 5 = 4? When investigating such things, encourage children to try ideas of their own to test out their ideas.

Equipment: *resource sheet (see page 78)*

TM

1 hexagon   2 triangle

MM

1 octagon

2 square

3 **a)** Listen to the children's predictions and reasons.

   b) (8-pointed star diagram)

   c) It is an 8-pointed star with an octagon in its centre. There are also triangles and kites to be found.

   Some children might find other shapes, e.g. square, pentagon and hexagon:

76   Supermaths Book 5

4 steps of 4 – straight line
   steps of 5 – 8-pointed star, which is the same as for steps of 3
   steps of 6 – square
   Some children might notice that the shape is formed in the opposite direction to the square formed by steps of 2.

5 a) 12-sided shape (dodecagon)   b) hexagon   c) square   d) triangle

6 steps of 6

7 a) and b) both look like this:

   They both look the same. Listen to the children's explanation of why, which might well include something about 5 and 7 both having a difference of 1 from the 'half way' 6.

8 steps of 8

9 Make a 12-sided shape that joins in the opposite direction to steps of 1.

10 Listen to the children's predictions.

11 The shapes that can be produced are:

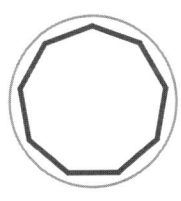

steps of: 1 and 8   2 and 7   3 and 6   4 and 5

Da Vinci files

a) pentagon   b) square
c) square   d) straight line
e) triangle   f) hexagon

a) anything where the step is either $\frac{1}{4}$ or $\frac{3}{4}$ of the number of dots
b) anything where the step is $\frac{1}{2}$ the number of dots
c) The dots will be a multiple of 7.
   If there are 7 dots, the step will be 3 or 4.
   If there are 14 dots, the step will be 6 or 8.
   If there are 21 dots, the step will be 9 or 12 and so on, with the step being the same multiple of 3 or 4 that the dots are a multiple of 7.

Mission File 5:1
Resource Sheet

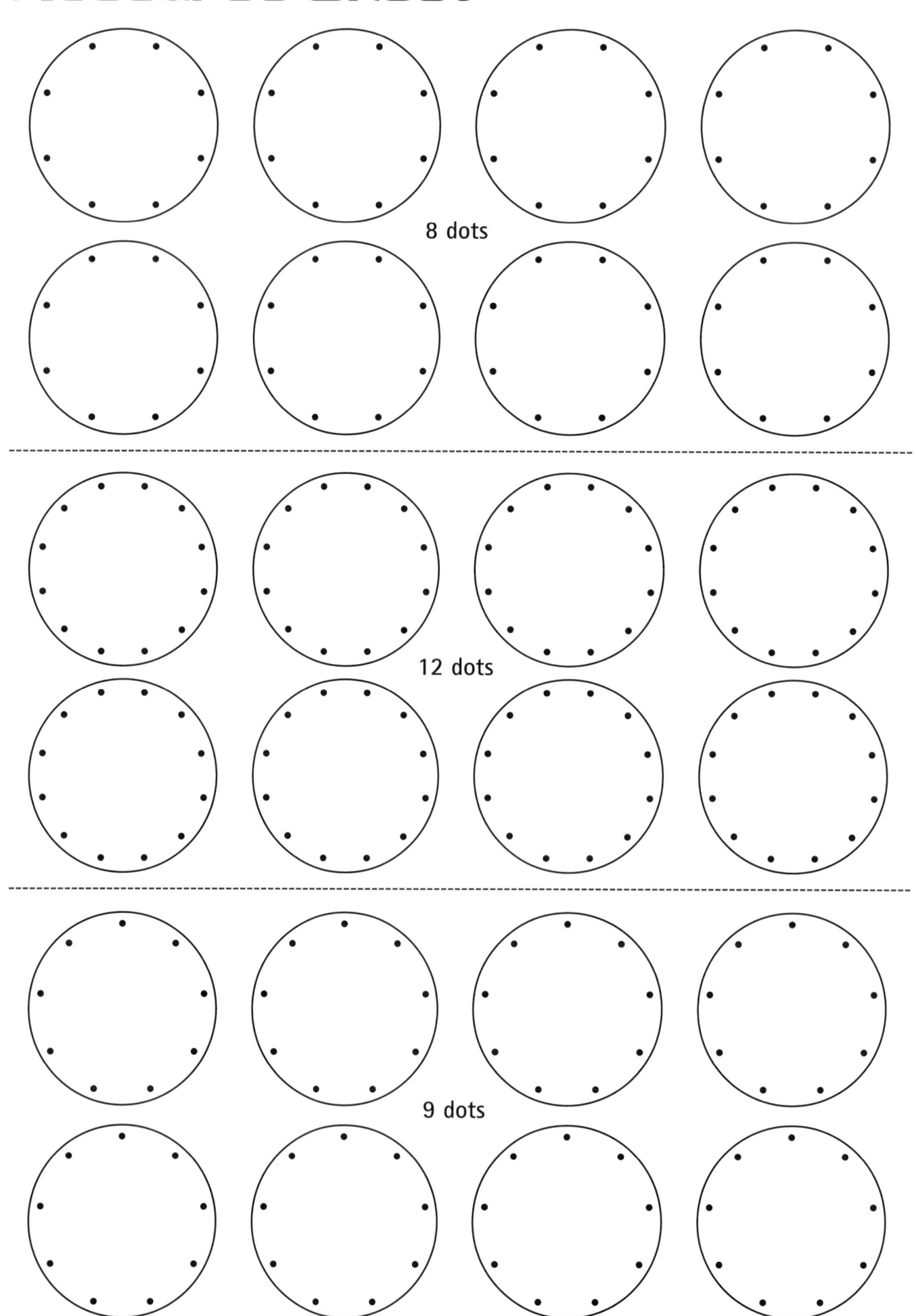

8 dots

12 dots

9 dots

78 Supermaths Book 5

Mission File 5:2
Cods-wallop's cocktails

Primary Framework Strands
- Using and applying mathematics
- Counting and understanding number

Teaching Content
- Proportion
- Ratio

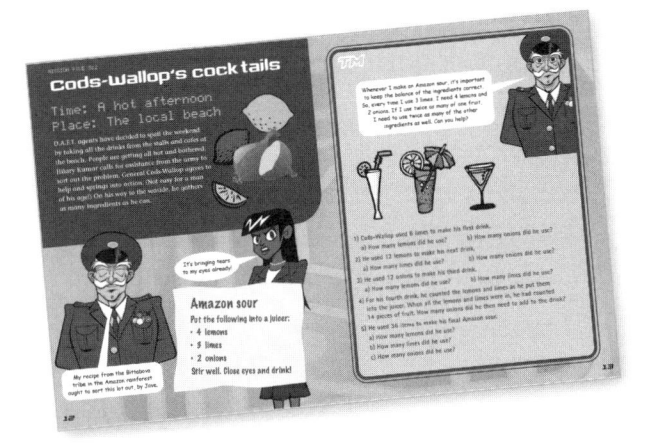

Teacher's Notes

In the TM, make sure that children understand how to scale items in the menu according to the information in the question. E.g. Where the menu uses 3 limes and the General uses 6, he must be making twice as much so all other ingredients must also be doubled.

TM question 4): make sure that the children understand that 14 is the total number of lemons AND limes used. This is twice the number used in the menu.

MM question 4): he could be using 6 or 7 times the numbers in the menu.

MM question 5): make sure the children realise that the numbers are being halved, not doubled.

TM

1 a) 8   b) 4
2 a) 9   b) 6
3 a) 24   b) 18
4 4
5 a) 16   b) 12   c) 8

MM

1 a) 15   b) 21
2 20
3 a) 25   b) 35   c) 15
4 a) 21   b) 30
5 a) 1.5 l   b) 2.5 l
6 20 l
7 a) 12 l   b) 20 l   c) 32 l
8 a) £192   b) £64 to the OB fund and £128 to the RG fund

Da Vinci files

24 Amazon sours
72 Spicy mango and passion-fruit punches
144 Orange and lime fizzers

Mission File 5:3
Industrial products

Primary Framework Strands
- Using and applying mathematics
- Knowing and using number facts

Teaching Content
- Multiples
- Products

Teacher's Notes

Children need to be familiar with the following terms: sum, total, product, difference, multiple and prime.

Some children may find the correct patterns and results but have difficulty expressing them appropriately. You may wish to display a word bank of suitable vocabulary or related examples as an aid.

While children should be allowed freedom to develop a logical approach to investigations where multiple options need to be assessed, if pupils are missing many options or losing track of which options they have tried, you may wish to suggest or demonstrate a more structured approach to the tasks.

The Da Vinci files can be extended by asking the children to consider numbers with 4, 5, 6 or more digits.

TM

1 **a)** all even   **b)** digits sum to a multiple of 3

   c) last 2 digits are divisible by 4 / half the number is even

   d) ends in 5 or 0   **e)** even and digit sum is a multiple of 3

2 All the answers are multiples of 3.

   They are all the product of 3 and the middle number of the three consecutive numbers.

   Suppose the 3 numbers are (a − 1), a and (a + 1)

   Adding gives: (a − 1) + a + (a + 1) = a − 1 + a + a + 1 = 3a

3 **a)** 1 + 1 + 1 + 1, 2 + 2

   minimum product is 1 × 1 × 1 × 1 = 1
   maximum product is 2 × 2 = 4
   yes: 1 × 1 × 2 = 2, 3 × 1 = 3

   b) 5 + 0, 4 + 1, 3 + 2, 3 + 1 + 1, 2 + 2 + 1
   2 + 1 + 1 + 1, 1 + 1 + 1 + 1 + 1
   minimum product is 1 × 1 × 1 × 1 × 1 = 1
   maximum product is 3 × 2 = 6
   no, you can't make 5

products for 6:
1 × 1 × 1 × 1 × 1 × 1 = 1
2 × 1 × 1 × 1 × 1 = 2, 3 × 1 × 1 × 1 = 3
4 × 1 × 1 = 4, 5 × 1 = 5, 3 × 2 × 1 = 6
4 × 2 = 8, 3 × 3 = 9
no, you can't make 7.

products for 7:
1 × 1 × 1 × 1 × 1 × 1 × 1 = 1
2 × 1 × 1 × 1 × 1 × 1 = 2, 3 × 1 × 1 × 1 × 1 = 3
4 × 1 × 1 × 1 = 4, 5 × 1 × 1 = 5, 6 × 1 = 6
4 × 2 × 1 = 8, 3 × 3 × 1 = 9
5 × 2 = 10, 3 × 4 = 12
no, you can't make 7 or 11.

Prime numbers that are equal to or more than the target number cannot be made.

MM

1 The non-zero minimum product is always 1 because all numbers can be created by adding 1s together and $1^n = 1$.

2 a)

Target Number	1	2	3	4	5	6	7	8	9	10
Sum for maximum product	1 + 0	1 + 1	2 + 1	2 + 2	3 + 2	3 + 3	3 + 4	3 + 3 + 2	3 + 3 + 3	3 + 3 + 4
Maximum Product	0	1	2	4	6	9	12	18	27	36

b) The sum for the maximum product consists of the digits 2, 3 and 4.

c) Rule example: add 3s together until you reach the target number or are either 2 or 4 short of it. Add 0, 2 or 4 as necessary.

d) 30 = 3 + 3 + 3 + 3 + 3 + 3 + 3 + 3 + 3 + 3
26 = 3 + 3 + 3 + 3 + 3 + 3 + 3 + 3 + 2

e)

Target number	Sum for maximum product	Maximum product	Difference in terms	Pattern in differences
1	1 + 0	0		
2	1 + 1	1	1	
3	1 + 2	2	1	
4	2 + 2	4	2	
5	3 + 2	6	2	
6	3 + 3	9	3	
7	3 + 4	12	3	1×3
8	3 + 3 + 2	18	6	2×3
9	3 + 3 + 3	27	9	3×3
10	3 + 3 + 4	36	9	$1 \times 9 = 1 \times 3^2$
11	3 + 3 + 3 + 2	54	18	$2 \times 9 = 2 \times 3^2$
12	3 + 3 + 3 + 3	81	27	$3 \times 9 = 3 \times 3^2$
13	3 + 3 + 3 + 4	108	27	$1 \times 27 = 1 \times 3^3$
14	3 + 3 + 3 + 3 + 2	162	54	$2 \times 27 = 2 \times 3^3$
15	3 + 3 + 3 + 3 + 3	243	81	$3 \times 27 = 3 \times 3^3$
16	3 + 3 + 3 + 3 + 4	324	81	$1 \times 81 = 1 \times 3^4$
17	3 + 3 + 3 + 3 + 3 + 2	486	162	$2 \times 81 = 2 \times 3^4$
18	3 + 3 + 3 + 3 + 3 + 3	729	243	$3 \times 81 = 3 \times 3^4$
19	3 + 3 + 3 + 3 + 3 + 4	972	243	$1 \times 243 = 1 \times 3^5$
20	3 + 3 + 3 + 3 + 3 + 3 + 2	1458	486	$2 \times 243 = 2 \times 3^5$

maximum product for sum of 25:
$1458 + (3 \times 3^5) + (1 \times 3^6) + (2 \times 3^6) + (3 \times 3^6) + (1 \times 3^7)$
$= 8748$

Da Vinci files

- 11, 22, 33, 44, 55, 66, 77, 88, 99, 110, 121
  When multiplying 11 by a 2-digit number, write the 2 digits with the unit digit in the units column and the tens digit in the hundreds column. Add the 2 digits and write the sum in the tens column, carrying as necessary.
  E.g. 23 × 11 gives H = 2, T = (2 + 3), U = 3; so the answer is 253
- 29th multiple is 29 × 11 = 319
  88th multiple is 88 × 11 = 968
- For 3-digit (or more) numbers, write the first digit a column to the left and the units digit in the units column. Add adjacent units to give the digits between, carrying as necessary.
  E.g. 463 × 11 = 4(4 + 6) (6 + 3)3 = 4(10)93 = 5093
  E.g. 53832 × 11 = 5(5 + 3)(3 + 8)(8 + 3)(3 + 2)2 = 58(11)(11)52 = 591(11)52 = 592152

- When multiplying by 9:
  up to and including the 10th multiple, subtract 1 from the multiple
  up to and including the 20th multiple, subtract 2 from the multiple
  up to and including the 30th multiple, subtract 3 from the multiple
  up to and including the 40th multiple, subtract 4 from the multiple and so on
  write the resulting number and then write the digit which takes the answer to the appropriate multiple of 9
  35 − 4 = 31, giving a digit sum of 4, so 5 is needed to total 9
- 35th multiple is 315
  74 − 8 = 66, giving a digit sum of 12, so 6 is needed to total 18
- 74th multiple is 666

Mission File 5:4

Pigs in paradise

Primary Framework Strands
- Using and applying mathematics

Teaching Content
- Measuring
- Area
- Pattern
- Prediction

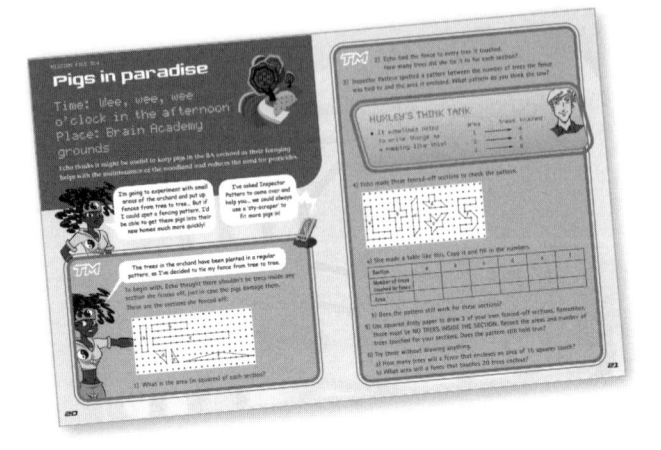

Teacher's Notes

When children are drawing their own shapes in the TM, encourage them to choose ones that might help them spot patterns. What happens if you increase the number of touching trees by 1, by 2, by 3 etc.?

In the MM, discuss why it is a good idea to only alter 1 thing at a time – either the number of touching trees or the number of trees inside – so that you know what effect the thing that is changing has. Many children (and adults) change everything in one go and then find it hard to spot relationships.

In the Da Vinci files, the inside trees make the most difference, so those are the ones to maximise. A carefully chosen scalene triangle will keep just 3 trees on the fence, leaving 9 for the inside.

This mission is based on Pick's theorem.

Equipment: *square dotty paper*

TM

1 a) 4   b) 6   c) 13
   d) 2   e) 1   f) 6

2 a) 10   b) 14   c) 28
   d) 6   e) 4   f) 14

3 Hopefully the pattern that the children spot will include some relationship between the number of trees touched and the area. It could be stated in many ways, including:
   - double the area and add 2 to get the number of trees $(a \times 2) + 2 = t$ or $2a + 2 = t$
   - add 1 to the area and then double to get the number of trees $(a + 1) \times 2 = t$ or $2(a + 1) = t$
   - halve the number of trees and then take away 1 to get the area $(t \div 2) - 1 = a$ or $\frac{1}{2}t - 1 = a$
   - take 2 from the number of trees and then halve to get the area $(t - 2) \div 2 = a$ or $\frac{1}{2}(t - 2) = a$

4 a)

Section	A	B	C	D	E	F
Number of trees touched by fence	18	16	12	10	11	21
Area	8	7	5	4	$4\frac{1}{2}$	$9\frac{1}{2}$

   b) The pattern still works as before.

82 Supermaths Book 5

5 Look at the children's own shapes. Check that they have not included any trees inside their shapes and that they have found the correct areas and number of trees on the boundary. If they have done this, then the pattern will still hold true.

6 a) 32 trees   b) 9 squares

MM

1

Section	A	B	C	D
Number of trees touched by fence	8	16	11	20
Number of trees inside section	1	3	10	8
Area	4	10	$14\frac{1}{2}$	17

2 a) Check that the children's drawings have 4 touching trees and 3, 4 and 5 trees inside.

b)

Section	A	B	C	D	E	F
Number of trees touched by fence	4	4	4	4	4	4
Number of trees inside section	0	1	2	3	4	5
Area	1	2	3	4	5	6

c) The area increases by 1 for each tree that is added inside.

3 Check that the children's drawings have 6 touching trees and 0, 1, 2, 3 and 4 trees inside.

Section	A	B	C	D	E
Number of trees touched by fence	6	6	6	6	6
Number of trees inside section	0	1	2	3	4
Area	2	3	4	5	6

The area increases by 1 for each tree that is added inside

4 The link the children spot should include some relationship between the number of trees touched (t), the number of trees inside (i) and the area (a). It could be stated in many ways, including:

halve the number of touched trees and take away 1 and then add the number of trees inside to get the area $\frac{1}{2}t - 1 + i = a$

take 2 from the number of touching trees and halve that number and then add the number of trees inside to get the area $\frac{1}{2}(t - 2) + i = a$

5 The link should still work as long as the children have counted things correctly.

6 a) 10 squares   b) $15\frac{1}{2}$ squares

7 Check the children's own drawings. They should match the criteria and areas shown in question 6.

Da Vinci Files

$9\frac{1}{2}$ squares (3 touching trees and 9 inside)

No, a total of 6 trees can only enclose $3\frac{1}{2}$ squares (3 touching trees and 3 inside).

Mission File 5:5

Bazza keeps an eye on things...

Primary Framework Strands
- Using and applying mathematics
- Calculating

Teaching Content
- Fractions
- Equivalence
- Simple addition

Teacher's Notes

Children might benefit from making fraction walls of some of the fractions involved in order to see the relationship between them.

Make sure that children are not repeating fractions in their answers – it's very easy to do that by mistake.

When changing a fraction into a sum of unit fractions, it is sometimes helpful to list some of the possible denominators.

TM

1 a) $\frac{1}{8} + \frac{1}{4} = \frac{3}{8}$ b) $\frac{1}{8} + \frac{1}{2} = \frac{5}{8}$ c) $\frac{1}{16} + \frac{1}{2} = \frac{9}{16}$ d) $\frac{1}{8} + \frac{1}{4} + \frac{1}{2} = \frac{7}{8}$

2 a) [eye symbol]   b) [eye symbol]   c) [symbol]

3 a) $\frac{5}{16}$ b) $\frac{13}{16}$ c) $\frac{3}{64}$

4 a) [eye symbol]   b) [eye symbol]   c) [symbol]

5 $\frac{63}{64}$

84 Supermaths Book 5

MM

1. a) $\frac{1}{8}$ b) $\frac{1}{16}$ c) $\frac{1}{4}$ d) $\frac{1}{4}$ $\frac{1}{8}$ $\frac{1}{16}$

2. a) $\frac{1}{3}$ b) $\frac{1}{4}$ c) $\frac{1}{3}$ $\frac{1}{12}$ d) $\frac{1}{3}$ $\frac{1}{9}$

3. Several ways are possible. The most likely are:

   a) $\frac{1}{2} + \frac{1}{6}$ b) $\frac{1}{2} + \frac{1}{10}$ c) $\frac{1}{3} + \frac{1}{9}$ d) $\frac{1}{2} + \frac{1}{5} + \frac{1}{10}$

4. a) The children's explanation should include something like:

   Put all the flour onto the balance, with some on both sides. Move the flour from one pan to the other until it balances.

   b) The children's explanation should halve as in (a) and then include something like:

   Take half the flour and put it on the balance. Move the flour from one pan to the other until it balances. That gives you quarters. Then either repeat with the other half or (better) balance some of the other half against one of the known quarters.

5. The children's explanation based on the addition $\frac{1}{2} + \frac{1}{4} + \frac{1}{8}$. Similar reasoning to question 4) but with an extra halving of quarters to get eighths.

6. The children's explanation based on the addition $\frac{1}{2} + \frac{1}{3}$. They may decide that the $\frac{1}{3}$ makes this not suitable for use with the balances.

Da Vinci files

Various answers are possible. Only some are shown here:

$\frac{3}{4} = \frac{1}{2} + \frac{1}{4}$ $\frac{3}{4} = \frac{1}{2} + \frac{1}{6} + \frac{1}{12}$

$\frac{3}{4} = \frac{1}{2} + \frac{1}{5} + \frac{1}{20}$ $\frac{3}{4} = \frac{1}{2} + \frac{1}{6} + \frac{1}{24} + \frac{1}{36} + \frac{1}{72}$

$\frac{3}{4} = \frac{1}{2} + \frac{1}{5} + \frac{1}{40} + \frac{1}{60} + \frac{1}{120}$

Yes it does for other fractions. It is always possible (though not always easy) to write one unit fraction as a sum of other unit fractions, so the last fraction can always be changed.

Mission File 5:6

Math-e-magics!

Primary Framework Strands
- Using and applying mathematics
- Calculating

Teaching Content
- Algebra

Teacher's Notes

Children will benefit from plenty of time to try these puzzles out and verify that they work. Make sure that they grasp that the answer is **always** the same (or always gives the required information).

It is useful for pupils to have a grasp of basic algebra to aid with the proofs. Check the children can write, using symbols and numbers, and expressions such as: n plus/minus 3, n multiplied by 4, (n + 4) multiplied by 5, and (2n + 6) divided by 2.

This mission gives an opportunity to stress the usefulness and importance of algebra in proving relationships and explaining things in maths.

Ensure that children understand the answer can be hidden in the answer. Making the puzzles can be tricky initially but soon becomes addictive. Children could be challenged to hide the information required in the answer.

TM

1 The answer is always 3.

Suppose the start number is N.

The steps are:

+ 3	N + 3
× 5	5N + 15
double	10N + 30
divide by 10	N + 3
subtract N	3

2 The answer is always 15

Suppose the start number is N.

The steps are:

+ 13	N + 13
× 2	2N + 26
− 6	2N + 20
halve	N + 10
add 5	N + 15
subtract N	15

86 Supermaths Book 5

MM

1 a) The original number is the difference between 10 and the given answer.

The steps are:

+ 20	N + 20
− P	N + 20 − P
× 10	10N + 200 − 10P
subtract 100	10N + 100 − 10P
halve	5N + 50 − 5P
divide by 5	N + 10 − P
subtract original number	10 − P

So whatever number is chosen as N, this shows that the final answer is always the difference between 10 and the number of people living in the house.

2 a) Children will get their own age and birth month as AAMM, e.g. 1103 is an 11-year-old born in March.

b) Mary 1304   Isaac 1111   Anne 1608   James 2412   Jaz 907

The digits in the thousands and hundreds columns give the age, the digits in the tens and units columns give the month of birth.

There may also be individual responses (not necessarily written down).

The steps are:

× 20	20A
+ 40	20A + 40
× 5	100A + 200
+ M	100A + 200 + M
− 200	100A + M

This shows that whatever number A is, it always ends up multiplied by 100, putting it into the hundreds and thousand columns; M is always added on, and since the maximum M is 12, it will be in the tens and units columns.

Da Vinci files

Check the algebra allows for a constant answer.

Check the algebra ends so that house number (*h*) can be easily identified.

Mission File 5:7
Speculate to tessellate

Primary Framework Strands
- Using and applying mathematics
- Understanding shape

Teaching Content
- Shape
- Tessellation
- Angles at a point
- Reasoning

Teacher's Notes

If the children find that their shape is not tessellating, encourage them to try different ways of arranging it because there will always be a way that works. Children sometimes tend to arrange shapes rather like petals of a flower, which can lead to awkward gaps.

In the MM, questions 6) to 9), make sure that the children understand the instructions for Huxley's method.

In the Da Vinci files, discuss that it must always work because the 4 corners of the quadrilateral are brought together each time. As the 4 corners of a quadrilateral always add up to 360°, the shapes will form a complete turn with no gaps. Continuing the method produces the same result at every point where shapes meet, so the tessellation will carry on forever.

Apply similar thinking to the triangles to see that the angles of any triangle must add up to 180°.

TM

1 The triangle tessellates.
Answers will vary. This is one example.

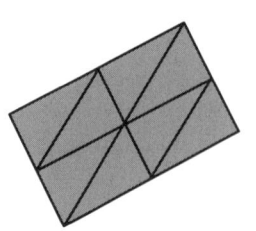

2 The triangles tessellate. Answers will vary. These are possible examples.
A   B

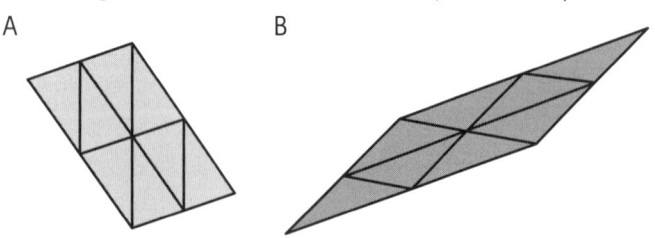

3 Look at the children's own triangle – it should tessellate.

4 All triangles will tessellate. See if the children have given reasons beyond talking about all the ones they have tried.

88 Supermaths Book 5

MM

1. The quadrilateral tessellates.
   Answers will vary. This is one example.

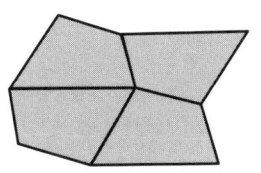

2. The quadrilaterals tessellate. Answers will vary. These are possible examples.

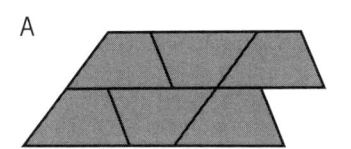

   A   B

3. Look at the children's own quadrilateral – it should tessellate.

4. It is impossible to make a quadrilateral that will not tessellate. If the children think they have, ask them to keep trying to tessellate it. Da Vinci files will eventually help with this!

5. All quadrilaterals will tessellate. See if the children have given reasons beyond talking about all the ones they have tried do.

6. **a)** Check that the children have drawn the tessellation according to the instructions.
   b) The left-hand side or the bottom side.
   c) The tessellation will continue.

7. Look at the children's own quadrilateral – it should tessellate.

8. It is impossible to make a quadrilateral that will not tessellate.

9. Huxley is right. See if the children have given reasons beyond talking about all the ones they have tried.

Da Vinci files

a) The 4 different symbols are around the points where four shapes meet.

b) As all 4 angles make a complete turn, the 4 angles of the quadrilateral add up to 360°

c) It is true for all quadrilaterals.

6 shapes meet at a point and the 3 different symbols appear twice each around the point. The 6 angles must total 360°, but as this is 2 lots of each angle, the 3 angles of the triangle must add up to 180°.

Mission File 5:8
Meet the aliens

Primary Framework Strands
- Using and applying mathematics
- Handling data

Teaching Content
- Probability

Teacher's Notes

You might want to check that children understand how to work out and record probabilities before starting this mission. You could use a group of children or objects on tray if needed.

To reduce the amount of recording necessary, children could be shown the shorthand method of writing probabilities. For example, p(H) could be used for 'the probability that the visitor wears a hat'.

The NOT, OR and AND rules are the main rules in probability. It is useful for pupils to gain experience in using these.

TM

Allow equivalent fractions.

1 a) $\frac{4}{10}$ b) $\frac{6}{10}$

2 a) $\frac{7}{10}$ b) $\frac{3}{10}$

3 a) $\frac{2}{10}$ b) $\frac{8}{10}$

4 a) $\frac{1}{10}$ b) $\frac{9}{10}$

5 The probabilities sum to one: P(have) + P(have not) = 1

6 a) $\frac{6}{8}$ b) $\frac{7}{12}$ c) $\frac{13}{20}$

7 Check the children's answers.

90 Supermaths Book 5

MM

1. a) $\frac{2}{15}$ b) $\frac{3}{15}$ or $\frac{1}{5}$ c) $\frac{5}{15}$ or $\frac{1}{3}$
2. a) $\frac{1}{15}$ b) $\frac{5}{15}$ or $\frac{1}{3}$ c) $\frac{6}{15}$ or $\frac{2}{5}$
3. a) $\frac{4}{15}$ b) $\frac{3}{15}$ or $\frac{1}{5}$ c) $\frac{7}{15}$
4. a) $\frac{2}{15}$ b) $\frac{5}{15}$ or $\frac{1}{3}$ c) $\frac{7}{15}$

5) The probability of having one attribute or another attribute is the sum of the probabilities of the individual attributes: p(A OR B) = p(A) + p(B)

    This is referred to as the 'OR' rule and it holds true when there are more than 2 options, so p(A OR B OR C) = p(A) + p(B) + p(C)

6. a) $\frac{5}{7}$ b) $\frac{12}{24}$ or $\frac{1}{2}$ c) Check the children's answers.

Da Vinci files

The probability that a spaceship will have both windows and wings is equal to 1 − (probability of not having windows) − (probability of not having wings). I.e. $1 - \frac{2}{6} - \frac{1}{6} = \frac{3}{6} = \frac{1}{2}$

Mission File 5:9

Beetle mania!

Primary Framework Strands
- Using and applying mathematics
- Understanding shape
- Measuring

Teaching Content
- Patterns
- Relationships

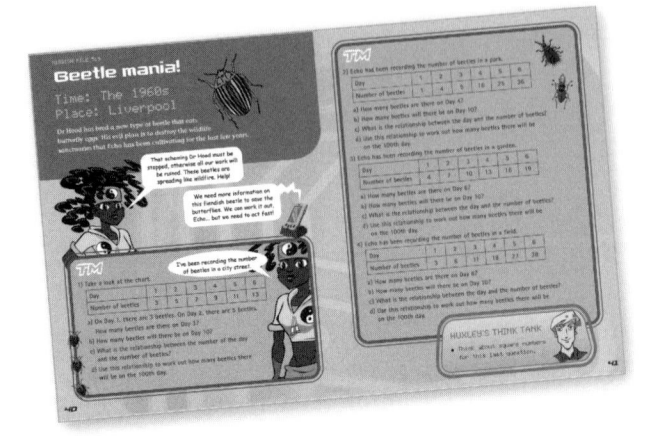

Teacher's Notes

This mission involves relating 2 sets of numbers – the day or week and the number of beetles. If the differences between the numbers of beetles are constant, the day is multiplied by the difference and the numbers added/subtracted as necessary. If the differences between the numbers of beetles are not constant, then usually the day needs to be squared and the answer adjusted with addition/subtraction.

Emphasise that accuracy in collecting the data is essential if a relationship is to be found.

TM

1. a) 7   b) 21   c) double the day and add 1: $2D + 1$ d) 201
2. a) 16 b) 100 c) square the day: D^2 d) 10,000
3. a) 19 b) 31   c) three times the day add 1: $3D + 1$ d) 301
4. a) 38 b) 102 c) square the day and add 2: $D^2 + 2$ d) 10,002

MM

1 **a)** Explanations such as:
   - the pattern starts with 1 and you add 3, then 5, then 7, then 9, 11, 13, 15...
   - the differences between the terms are 3, 5, 7, 9, 11...
   - the terms are square numbers

   b) The number contaminated is the square of the number of weeks.

   c) $T = W^2$

   d) 63.24 weeks (allow 64 weeks but not 63 weeks)

2 **a)** $T = 6W^2$

   b) 25.82 weeks (allow 26 weeks but not 25 weeks)

Da Vinci files

Squares: double the week, subtract 1 and square the answer $(2W - 1)^2$
Triangles: $6W^2 - 6W + 1$
Two triangle rhombus: $6W^2 - 4W$
Three triangle trapezium: $6W^2 - 2W - 1$

The TASC wheel

**All children can learn to be better thinkers.
They just need to practise the <u>strategies</u> of expert thinkers!**

Learn from experience
Children need to think about their learning.
Talking about what they have learned extends mental maps and connects ideas.

Gather/organise
Ask the children to gather together what they already know. This can be oral or jotted down quickly in a flow chart or mind map. This process gathers information stored in the memory and brings it into the working memory ready for action.

Identify
Ask the children to explain the task in their own words. Ask them to highlight the key words.
This helps to clarify the task and to focus on the key elements.

Communicate
Children need to share their thinking – sharing is a celebration!
Telling someone else clarifies the process of problem-solving.

Generate
Even if there is a conventional 'right answer', encourage the children to think of other possible solutions.
Always encourage creative thinking and develop their self-confidence to explore possibilities.

Evaluate
Let the children decide whether they were successful. Encourage rethinking and revisions.
Emphasise that 'mistakes' are good learning points. Encourage self-appraisal and self-assessment.

Implement
The children can work orally or with quick sketches, flowcharts or mind maps.
Maximum thinking and talking! Minimum necessary recording!

Decide
Let the children decide on the strategy they will use.
This encourages decision-making and self-confidence.
This prioritises action!

TASC: Thinking Actively in a Social Context © Belle Wallace 2004

nace

Advancing teaching...
Inspiring able learners every day
www.nace.co.uk

NACE exists to support the daily work of teachers providing for pupils of high ability whilst enabling all pupils to flourish. It is an independent charity, founded in 1984.

We promote:
- the fact that able, gifted and talented children and young people have particular educational needs which must be met to realise their potential
- the use of differentiated educational provision through curriculum enrichment and extension
- education as an enjoyable, exciting and worthwhile experience for the able, gifted and talented.

We are a large association of professionals offering a wealth of experience in working with more able pupils. We provide advice, training and materials on learning and teaching, leadership and management and whole-school improvement to schools and LEAs. Our publications are the seminal and most comprehensive series of books about able, gifted and talented education.

Our partnership with Rising Stars enables us to provide books which reflect our principles of learning by engaging able pupils in:
- thinking and working creatively to solve practical problems
- learning from mistakes and seeing themselves in control of their learning
- working independently and with others
- expecting to progress to the next level of mastery
- behaving and thinking as an expert

NACE membership includes schools, corporate bodies and individuals. Members are teachers, headteachers, school coordinators, LEA advisors and officers, Ofsted Inspectors, psychologists, researchers, HMI, university and college staff, school governors, parents and educators from overseas.

NACE is an independent organisation with regular contacts with national bodies such as the DCFS, Ofsted, QCA, ACCAC, TDA, BECTA and the National Academy for Gifted and Talented Youth. Internationally, NACE is affiliated to the European Council for High Ability and the World Council for Gifted and Talented Children.

NACE National Office, PO Box 242, Arnolds Way, Oxford OX2 9FR
T: 01865 861879 f: 01865 861880 e: info@nace.co.uk www.nace.co.uk
Registered Charity No: 327230